SPHERE RIG

Harjit Grewal read Law
tising barrister. She was
Relations Committee, chaired by Lord Justice Browne-
Wilkinson (as he then was), which investigated and
reported on race discrimination within the Bar in
1983.

Other titles in the *Sphere Rights Guides* series:

Forthcoming:

SPHERE RIGHTS GUIDES
Series editor: Andrew Arden

THE RACE DISCRIMINATION HANDBOOK

HARJIT GREWAL

SPHERE REFERENCE

SPHERE BOOKS LTD

Published by the Penguin Group
27 Wrights Lane, London W8 5TZ, England
Viking Penguin Inc., 40 West 23rd Street, New York, New York 10010, USA
Penguin Books Australia Ltd, Ringwood, Victoria, Australia
Penguin Books Canada Ltd, 2801 John Street, Markham, Ontario, Canada L3R 1B4
Penguin Books (NZ) Ltd, 182–190 Wairau Road, Auckland 10, New Zealand

Penguin Books Ltd, Registered Offices: Harmondsworth, Middlesex, England

First published by Sphere Books Ltd 1988

Printed and bound in Great Britain by
Richard Clay Ltd, Bungay, Suffolk

Contents

Contents

Contents

8: Proceedings in the County Court   96

Contents

Contents

Publisher's Note

The law can change at short notice. This book describes the law on racial discrimination as at 29 February 1988. You should always check if what it says is still correct.

1: The Meaning of Racial Discrimination

What is racial discrimination?
Discrimination, as defined by the law, can occur in one of two ways: it can be either direct or indirect. If you are discriminated against on racial grounds, then it is racial discrimination. Racial grounds are those of your colour, race, nationality (and that includes citizenship) or ethnic or national origins, or because you belong to a racial group defined by reference to one of these factors.

What is direct discrimination?
Direct discrimination is quite straightforward; it simply means that you are being treated less favourably than others (in the same position as you) are actually treated or would be treated, and the reason for it is one or more of the following – your colour, race, nationality or ethnic or national origins.

Although it is easy to understand what direct discrimination means, it is quite another matter trying to prove it. Those who treat you less favourably on racial grounds are hardly likely to admit that they have done so. In determining whether racial discrimination has taken place, courts and tribunals will examine the reasons given by the discriminator for any less favourable treatment and see if they are in fact the real reasons.

The following are examples of what may amount to direct discrimination:

A black woman with a British-sounding name applies

for a job. When she arrives for the interview she is told that the vacancy has already been filled. The next day she sees an advertisement in a newspaper for the same job. In the absence of a satisfactory and credible explanation by the employer for the lie that had been told, a tribunal would decide that discrimination had taken place.

An Indian man seeks entrance to a night club. He is refused on the grounds that the club is full. Ten minutes later he sees a white man being allowed into the club. Again, in the absence of a satisfactory explanation, this would be held to be discrimination.

What is indirect discrimination?

Indirect discrimination is slightly more complicated. It takes place if someone imposes a 'requirement' or 'condition' which, on the face of it, has nothing to do with race or colour and appears to apply equally to everyone. However, in reality, the condition is such that the proportion of your racial group who can comply with it is considerably smaller than the proportion of other racial groups. If there is no justification for it and you are adversely affected because you cannot comply with it, this is indirect discrimination against you.

An example of this might be where a school has a rule that all pupils must wear a particular cap as part of the school uniform. X is an orthodox Sikh and wears long hair under a turban; he, therefore, cannot comply with this rule. As a result he is refused admission to the school. Unless the school can show this rule to be justifiable, X has suffered indirect discrimination.

Two important factors must be borne in mind. First, the question is not whether an individual can in *theory* comply with the rule, but whether he can do so in *practice*. In the above example it is of course theoretically possible for X to discard his turban, cut his hair short and wear the school cap. However, he cannot do so in practice unless he abandons the traditions, customs and culture of his racial group. In those circumstances he is perfectly entitled to say that he cannot comply with the rule.

Second, you can only complain of indirect discrimination if you are actually affected by it. If, in the above example, X had been a Sikh who had short hair and did not wear a turban, he would not have been entitled to complain about the rule.

What is meant by a 'requirement' or 'condition'?

A requirement or condition simply means a 'must' – something which has to be complied with. It must be such that your failure to comply with it would mean that you could never get whatever it was that you wanted.

A simple example illustrates the point. X, a man born in India, who qualified and practised as a barrister there, applies for a legal post in this country. The only requirement for the post is that the applicant must be a qualified barrister. In assessing the suitability of candidates, the interviewing board takes into account a variety of factors, one of which is command of the English language. X learnt English as a second language and is not very fluent in it. He is refused the job because he does not rate very highly on any of the factors taken into account. Although the proportion of barristers born and qualified in India who would have a good command of the English language is smaller than the proportion of barristers born and qualified in the United Kingdom, X could not succeed in a claim for indirect discrimination because poor English is not a factor which excludes him from ever getting such a job.

When is a discriminatory condition justifiable?

Once you have established that a condition exists – that the proportion of your racial group who can comply with it is smaller than the proportion of other racial groups who can comply with it, *and* that it is detrimental to you – then it is for the person imposing the condition to prove that it is justifiable, notwithstanding its obvious discriminatory effect.

There is no special rule or formula to apply when deciding whether a particular condition is justifiable or not. If a condition has been imposed simply to suit the convenience or personal preference of the person imposing it, that is *not* enough to make it justifiable. On the other hand, the person imposing it does not have to go so far as to show that it is *absolutely* necessary. In the grey area that lies between these two extremes, the question of whether a condition is justifiable will depend upon the facts of your individual case.

The following two examples illustrate the kind of approach taken by the courts when deciding this issue.

The head teacher of a Christian school has a rule that all pupils must wear a school cap, thus making it impossible for a turbaned Sikh to join the school. Two reasons are put forward as justification for this rule. First, the practical convenience of having a school uniform (for instance, it minimizes external differences between pupils of different races and social classes). Second, as this is a Christian school the head teacher objects to the turban on the ground that it is an outward manifestation of a non-Christian faith. In these circumstances, the rule is *not* justifiable.

A chocolate factory has a rule that employees must be clean-shaven. An orthodox Sikh with a beard is refused a job at the factory unless he shaves off his beard. The factory contends that the rule is justifiable on the grounds of hygiene and public health. They call evidence to show that if hair from a person's beard were to fall into the food being manufactured, not only would it be disagreeable and give rise to complaints from customers about the nature of the food, but it would also carry with it a risk of bacteria being transmitted to the food and of people suffering illness or disease as a result. In such a case the rule would be justifiable. In fact, where issues of public health are concerned, so long as they are supported by scientific evidence, a condition will almost invariably be justifiable.

What if I am discriminated against because of my religion?

Discrimination on religious grounds is not specifically covered by the Race Relations Act 1976, and thus it is not unlawful. However, what may initially appear to be religious discrimination may in fact be discrimination on one of the racial grounds as set out in the Act – that is on the basis of your colour, race, nationality, or ethnic or national origins, or because you belong to a particular racial group which is defined by reference to one of these factors.

Discrimination because you belong to a certain ethnic group is the most common because 'ethnic' has been given a relatively wide meaning by the courts. 'An ethnic group' has been defined as a group of people which regards itself and is regarded by others as a distinct community by virtue of certain characteristics, two of which are essential. First, it must have a long shared history, of which the group is conscious as distinguishing it from other groups, the memory of which it keeps alive. Second, it must have a cultural tradition of its own, including family and social customs and manners, often but not necessarily associated with religious observances. In addition, the following characteristics could also be relevant. A common geographical origin or descent from a small number of common ancestors; a common language (which does not necessarily have to be exclusive to the group); a common literature which is particular to the group; a common religion different from that of neighbouring groups or from the general community surrounding it; and the characteristics of being a minority or an oppressed group within a larger community.

If these criteria are applied, then Sikhs and Jews constitute distinct ethnic groups, and discrimination against them amounts to discrimination on racial grounds.

Is discrimination against gypsies discrimination on racial grounds?

Yes, because they are a distinct ethnic group.

Are the motives and intentions of the discriminator a relevant consideration?

The correct approach is to look at the factual nature of the act itself. The question to be asked is – has there been less favourable treatment and is the reason for it the colour, race, etc. of the individual concerned? If so, it will be racial discrimination even though the person responsible did not mean to discriminate on racial grounds and may, indeed, have had the best possible motives for the action that he or she took. It is no defence to an allegation of racial discrimination to say, 'I did not want to discriminate. I am entirely against racial discrimination, but the racial prejudice of others forced me to take the course I did.'

For example, a restaurant employs a black waitress for the first time. The owner then finds that customers are no longer using the restaurant, that the black employee is being subjected to abuse, and there is a risk that the business may collapse. The owner, therefore, reluctantly sacks the black employee, partly motivated by a desire to save the business from collapse and perhaps even partly to save the black employee from further distressing incidents. Despite having relatively decent motives, the employer is nevertheless treating the black employee less favourably on racial grounds and is therefore guilty of racial discrimination.

Similarly, someone may impose a requirement or condition without ever considering or realizing its likely effect upon a particular racial group, let alone intending to discriminate against them. If, however, the effect is discriminatory and it cannot be justified, that person will be guilty of racial discrimination. For instance, the head teacher who insists that all pupils must wear a school cap as part of the uniform may have had the best possible motives, such as the removal of social and class barriers between children and an attempt to promote a feeling of equality between them. It is nevertheless racial discrimination because the effect of it is to exclude boys of a particular ethnic group, namely Sikhs.

It is important, however, to remember that in a case of indirect discrimination no damages will be awarded if there was no intention to discriminate (see pages 54 and 103).

What if race is not the only reason for my being treated less favourably?

A person's conduct may still amount to racial discrimination even though race is not the *only* ground on which you are being treated less favourably.

However, in order to succeed in a claim for racial discrimination you would have to prove that race was a 'substantial' and 'effective' cause for the action which the person took – in other words, that it was a major reason for the person's behaviour, and not just an incidental factor.

It is important to remember that if you are a black woman, you may be discriminated against not only on racial grounds but also because of your sex. In such a situation you are entitled to bring a claim for *both* race *and* sex discrimination. (For the law on sex discrimination, see *The Sex Discrimination Handbook*, also available in this series.)

Taking proceedings for race discrimination does not prevent you from taking other proceedings. It may often be appropriate to bring one action alleging various forms of unlawful conduct. For instance, if you have been employed for over two years and are dismissed for racial reasons, you may be entitled to bring proceedings for unfair dismissal in addition to bringing proceedings for race discrimination.

What if I am discriminated against because of someone else's race or colour?

If A discriminates against B because of C's colour, race, etc., then A's conduct amounts to racial discrimination against B, who can bring proceedings against A for it. Thus if a publican refuses to serve a white woman because she is accompanied by a black man, then that publican is discriminating against *her* on racial grounds, and *she* is entitled to bring proceedings against the publican.

The same applies if a publican instructs a bar worker not to serve black customers, and the bar worker's refusal to comply with this order leads to dismissal. It is unlawful to instruct others to discriminate, but that is a matter in respect of which only the Commission for Racial Equality can take proceedings (see Chapter 10). Although the bar worker is not treated less favourably because of his or her *own* race or colour, the publican is nevertheless guilty of race discrimination for treating the bar worker less favourably on racial grounds, i.e. the race of others.

Does segregation amount to racial discrimination?

Racial segregation means the separation or keeping apart of people of different races or colour. The mere fact that there is segregation does not necessarily mean that racial discrimination is taking place. Segregation amounts to racial discrimination only if it takes place deliberately, that is, because of a specific policy or decision to keep persons of different races apart.

For instance, if a restaurant owner deliberately seats black customers in a separate room from white customers in the belief that the presence of the former will offend the latter, the owner is guilty of racial discrimination. If, however, the black customers prefer to sit among themselves and away from the white customers, and therefore always sit in a separate room, then the 'factual segregation' does not amount to race discrimination. In such a situation it is not incumbent upon anyone to take steps to prevent the segregation taking place.

Similarly, if an employer has a policy of keeping Asian workers apart from others and, consequently, the personnel department sends all the Asians taken on – and only the Asians – to a particular part of the workplace, that is racial discrimination. If, however, there are only Asians in a particular part of the workplace because whenever vacancies arise in that part they are filled by people introduced by those already working there, and for that reason they are of the same race, that is not racial discrimination. In circumstances such as these, the failure of the company to have a more positive employment policy, which would have removed any element of segregation, would not be held to be race discrimination.

What if I am victimized for being involved in race discrimination proceedings?

You can bring proceedings for race discrimination against anyone who treats you less favourably than they treat or would treat others in similar circumstances, and does so for any of the following reasons:

(a) You have brought proceedings for racial discrimination against either them or someone else.

(b) You have given evidence or information in connection with any proceedings for racial discrimination (it does not matter if the *information* was given before any proceedings were actually begun so long as the victimization occurred at a time when proceedings had actually been brought, and the reason for it was the giving of the information).

(c) You have done something 'by reference to' the Race Relations Act 1976. Doing something 'by reference to' the Act means, for example, making a report to the Commission for Racial Equality or to a Community Relations Council that facts are available which ought to be investigated and which indicate a possible breach of the Race Relations Act 1976.

(d) You have alleged that someone has done something which, assuming your allegation to be true, would amount to racial discrimination.

(e) The person treating you less favourably knows that you intend to do any of the above things (in paragraphs (a)–(d)) or suspects that you have done or intend to do any of them.

If, however, you are being treated less favourably because of an allegation made by you, and your allegation was in fact false and not made by you in good faith, then you cannot complain that you have been discriminated against by way of victimization.

Is every act of race discrimination unlawful?

No. The Race Relations Act 1976 specifies particular types of behaviour in certain fields which amount to unlawful race discrimination. Once you have established that you have been discriminated against – directly, indirectly, or by way of victimization – the next question is whether the discrimination is unlawful.

Certain discriminatory conduct in relation to employment (see Chapters 2 and 3), education (see Chapter 5), housing and other premises (see Chapter 6), the provision of goods, facilities and services, and membership of associations (see Chapter 7) is unlawful discrimination.

It is important to realize that the law can only provide remedies for acts of unlawful discrimination. It cannot in any way deal with racist beliefs and attitudes. Racial prejudice in itself is not against the law; the law can only intervene and assist you if that prejudice is translated into some kind of unlawful discriminatory act.

2: Discrimination by Employers

Who is an employer?

For the purposes of race discrimination, an employer is someone who hires people to work for him or her either under a contract of service or apprenticeship or under a contract personally to execute any work or labour.

Being hired under 'a contract of service' simply means that you are working for the person concerned as their employee, as opposed to doing work for them in your capacity as a self-employed person. The question of whether you are an employee or a self-employed person will depend on all the circumstances of your working relationship. The presence of the following factors would tend to show that you are an employee: a certain degree of control over how and when you do your work; a fixed remuneration paid at regular intervals; the fact that you are tied to one employer and are not free to work for others; the fact that income tax and national insurance contributions are paid directly by the employer; and the fact that the working relationship can be terminated by dismissal. In order to determine this question all aspects of the relationship have to be considered, as no single factor is in itself decisive.

'A contract personally to execute any work or labour' is a wide and flexible term and may in some situations include self-employed persons. In order to determine whether you are employed under such a contract, two questions have to be answered. First, whether your duties constitute work or labour, and, second, the extent to which you are required to execute the duties yourself. You must be under an obligation to do some part of the work yourself, and not merely be responsible for seeing that the work is carried out. There is no strict rule as to the precise degree of personal involvement required in the execution of work to bring it within the definition. On one hand, the smallest element of personal involvement will not necessarily bring a contract within the definition; on the other hand, you do not have to go so far as to show that all the work will be carried out by you personally. Whether your contract comes within the definition will depend on all the facts of your case.

Against whom must an employer not discriminate?

It is unlawful for an employer to discriminate racially against those who work for him, those who are looking for work (this includes job applicants) and 'contract workers'.

You are a 'contract worker' if you are employed by A (the employer) who in turn sends you out to work for B. You do not have any contract with B and B is not legally your employer. It is nevertheless unlawful for B to discriminate racially against you. For example, you are a black secretary working for a temp agency. You are sent to work for two weeks with the manager of a company. Upon seeing you, the manager tells you that you are not suitable for the job and asks the agency to send someone else. That is unlawful discrimination and you can bring proceedings against the manager, even though you are employed by someone else.

Can an employer discriminate if the job is overseas?

Race discrimination is unlawful *only* in relation to employment at an establishment in Great Britain. An employer in this country is therefore permitted to discriminate on racial grounds if the job is such that the work is or will be done wholly or mainly outside Britain. For instance, a British company based in London is hiring engineers to work on a project in South Africa. It does not break the law if it refuses, as a matter of policy, to hire black engineers. Alternatively, if it hired black engineers from this country, it would not be breaking the law if it paid the black engineers less than their white colleagues. It would, however, be unlawful for the company to advertise for white engineers only (see page 111).

If the job involves working on a British ship, aircraft or hovercraft, an employer can discriminate only if the work is, or will be, done *wholly* outside Britain. If *any* part of the work is done in this country, race discrimination is unlawful. For example, if you work on a British ship and are paid less because of your colour, that is permitted so long as the ship never enters British territorial waters. If it does, then discrimination against you is unlawful, even if it took place while you were in the Pacific. If, however, the discrimination relates to recruitment in this country, it will not be unlawful if at the relevant time it was not contemplated that the ship would dock at a British port, even if it subsequently does so.

What is unlawful discrimination when I am looking for a job?

If you are looking for a job, it is unlawful for an employer to discriminate racially against you either by not offering you the job or by offering it to you on less favourable terms than to other applicants or employees.

The refusal to offer you the job can occur in a variety of ways. You may be interviewed but not offered the job although your qualifications and experience make you a more suitable candidate than anyone else; you may arrive for an interview and be told that the vacancy has already been filled; you may not be invited for an interview at all; your application may not even be acknowledged.

One of the reasons for your not being offered the job may be that the employer has made discriminatory arrangements for recruiting. This in itself is unlawful. 'Discriminatory arrangements for recruiting' covers a wide variety of matters and may include discriminatory advertising (see page 110), discriminatory instructions to employment agencies or a personnel department (see page 113), discouraging you from applying for the job on some other pretext, or imposing requirements and/or selection criteria that are not related to the safe and effective performance of the job and are discriminatory.

An employer will have acted unlawfully if you are not offered a job for any of the following reasons:

(a) The employer required a higher standard of English than was necessary for the particular job.

(b) The employer used selection and aptitude tests that had no bearing on the job and put people not born or brought up in this country at a disadvantage. For example, applicants for a purely clerical post are assessed on their ability to answer general knowledge questions on English history.

(c) The employer imposed a condition that applicants must have been born in the UK or have lived here for a certain number of years (for the exception to this, see page 24).

(d) The employer indicated that overseas degrees and diplomas, even when comparable with UK qualifications, would not be recognized.

(e) The employer stipulated certain conditions that were unjustified as to dress or appearance. For instance, a department store requires all female sales assistants to wear a navy-blue skirt, brown tights and black shoes. A

Pakistani woman applying for the job asks if she may wear trousers as it is part of her traditional culture not to expose her legs. The store refuses and she is not offered the job. The proportion of Pakistani women who can comply with the uniform requirement is smaller than the proportion of English women who can comply with it. The imposing of this requirement is, therefore, indirect race discrimination.

An offer of a job to you on less favourable terms than to others is unlawful, even if you do not accept the offer. Your terms of employment cover such things as your pay, working hours and conditions, time off for holidays and sickness, perks that go with the job (such as a company car, commission and expenses), and pensions and death benefits. Thus it is unlawful to offer to pay a black employee less than white employees doing the same job, or to insist that black employees work anti-social hours (such as doing night shifts) or in more unsavoury conditions.

What is unlawful discrimination at my workplace?

Your employer must not, on racial grounds, treat you less favourably than other employees. This means that:

(a) You must not be employed on less favourable terms than other employees. For examples of terms of employment, see the answer to the last question.)

(b) You must not be treated less favourably in relation to promotion, transfer or training (that includes any form of education or instruction). Thus an employer acts unlawfully if he or she overlooks a senior and experienced black employee for promotion to a higher post, and promotes instead a junior and less able and experienced white employee. The black employee's case is strengthened if a black person has never held the higher post.

(c) An employer must not treat you less favourably in affording you access to any benefits, facilities or services. For example, you work for a travel agency and learn from your white colleagues that all employees are entitled to buy air tickets for ten per cent of their normal price. You ask your employer about it and are told that there is no such rule, although you know it is a benefit the white employees have had. The affording of access to benefits, facilities and services is not limited to those provided by the employer, but includes any means by which it is in the employer's power to facilitate access to benefits, facilities and services provided by any other person.

If, however, your employer provides benefits, facilities or services to the public at large, or to a section of it, you may have been discriminated against as a member of the public, as opposed to as an employee. You will have been discriminated against as an employee if there was a material difference between the benefits etc. provided to the public and those provided to you; *or* if the provision of benefits etc. was regulated by your contract of employment; *or* if the benefits etc. related to your training.

If you have been discriminated against as a member of the public, you can still bring legal proceedings, but they are different from the proceedings you bring as an employee. As an employee you would bring proceedings in an industrial tribunal (see Chapter 4). As a member of the public you would have to bring proceedings in a County Court (see Chapters 7 and 8).

(d) You must not be dismissed on racial grounds. For example, an Asian employee is involved in a fight at the workplace, and the employer's response is to sack *all* the Asian employees.

If you are dismissed, you may in some circumstances

be entitled to bring proceedings for unfair dismissal as well as for race discrimination.

(e) You must not be subjected to any other detrimental treatment, as in the following examples: an employer is frequently racially abusive; a black employee at a department store is caught stealing and is dismissed, so the store makes it a rule that all black employees leaving the shop must be searched; an employer has to make ten employees redundant and all those selected for redundancy are black, although some of them have been in employment far longer than their white workmates; or the employer discriminates in the operation of grievance, disputes and disciplinary procedures (for instance, a black employee and a white employee both arrive drunk for work and as a result the black employee is suspended, while the white is not).

What is unlawful discrimination against contract workers?

It is unlawful for the 'principal' (your temporary employer) to discriminate racially against you in any of the following ways:

(a) By allowing you to do your work on less favourable terms than others in the same position as you but of different race.

(b) By not allowing you to do the work or to continue doing it.

(c) By denying you access to any benefits, facilities or services, or by giving you restricted access to them. It may be that you are being denied or given restricted access as a member of the public as opposed to as a contract worker (see page 17).

What if I am discriminated against by other employees?

An employer is liable for the acts of employees which are done in the course of their employment, whether or not they are done with that employer's approval or knowledge. In such a situation, an employer will not be liable if it can be shown that he or she took such steps as were reasonably practicable to prevent the discrimination from taking place. Whether your employer took 'such steps as were reasonably practicable' will depend on the facts of your particular case.

In the following examples, the employer would be liable for the employees' acts of discrimination.

A restaurant owner knows that the manager discriminates against black applicants when recruiting waiters. The employer tells the manager once that this should not be done, but then takes no further steps to ensure that racial discrimination does not occur, although the waiting staff continues to be all white. If thereafter you apply for a job and are discriminated against by the manager, you can bring proceedings against the owner.

As a black employee, you are frequently racially abused by your white colleagues, and have occasionally been assaulted by them. You complain several times to the management but your complaints are never investigated and no action is taken against the white employees. The company is liable for the racist behaviour of its employees, and you can bring proceedings for race discrimination against it.

Is race discrimination by employers ever allowed by law?

Yes. Discrimination by employers is not unlawful if it takes place in any of the following circumstances:

Private households

A person can lawfully discriminate against employees, or in recruitment, if the employment in question is for the purposes of a private household. However, an employer may not *victimize* any employee for having been involved in race discrimination proceedings. Thus, an employer who dismisses a maid for giving information about discrimination by the employer in his or her office is guilty of unlawful discrimination, while one who refuses to employ a maid simply because she is black is not. Similarly, it is allowable to pay a black maid less than a white one.

Employment can be for the purposes of a private household even though the employer is a company or some other institution, such as where a company employs a butler or cook to work in the home of a senior member of staff. The employment must, however, be either wholly or at least to a substantial degree for the purposes of a private household. Thus, a chauffeur who is employed by a company primarily to drive the managing director to and from work is not employed for the purposes of a private household, even though the chauffeur may be for part of the day at the disposal of the director's family.

Genuine occupational qualification

An employer may lawfully discriminate in recruitment or in giving employees the opportunity for promotion, transfer or training, if it can be shown that it is an essential requirement for the job in question that the person doing it be of a particular racial group.

There are only four circumstances in which an employer can claim that being of a particular colour, race, nationality or ethnic group is a genuine occupational qualification. Some or all of the duties of the job *must* fall into one of the following categories:

(a) The job is to play a particular role in a film or a play which requires the person to be of a particular racial group for reasons of authenticity. Thus it is perfectly lawful for a theatre production to audition only black actors when looking for someone to play Othello, or for a film company to look for a white actor to play President Kennedy in a film about his life.

(b) The job involves participation as an artist's or photographic model in the production of a work of art or a visual image which requires the person to be of a particular racial group for reasons of authenticity.

(c) The job involves working in a restaurant, bar or café, the setting of which requires, for reasons of authenticity, persons of a particular racial group to work in it. This would apply, for example, to a Chinese restaurant employing only Chinese waiters.

(d) The job involves providing persons of a particular racial group with personal services promoting their welfare, and the job can be carried out most effectively by a person of the same racial group. For example, it is lawful for an Asian women's refuge (a home for battered women) to employ Asian workers on the basis that Asian women would find it easier to relate to and communicate with Asian workers.

Employers cannot argue that they employed someone of a particular racial group for any of the reasons given above if they already have, at that time, employees of that racial group who were capable of carrying out the relevant duties, whom it would have been reasonable to employ on those duties and whose numbers were sufficient to meet the likely requirements in respect of those duties without undue inconvenience.

Training of people from overseas
An employer acts lawfully in discriminating positively in order to provide training skills for people not

ordinarily resident in Britain if it appears to the employer that the skills thus provided will be used wholly outside Britain. It does not matter if the person in question subsequently settles and uses those skills in Britain. What is important is the employer's understanding of that person's intentions at the time of employment. For example, a British company makes a contract with the Indian government to sell them machinery that is made in Britain, and a term of the contract is that a certain number of Indians come to work at the British plant and be trained to use and maintain the machinery. An English person who does not get a job at the plant cannot complain of race discrimination.

Seamen recruited abroad

A seaman cannot complain of discrimination in connection with working on a ship if he applied or was engaged for the job outside Britain. A recruit brought to Britain to sign an employment agreement is still treated as having been recruited abroad. Even when a ship is in British territorial waters, discrimination against seamen recruited abroad is permitted.

Positive discrimination in training

An employer may positively discriminate in favour of members of a particular racial group by training them for certain posts or encouraging them to apply for them *only if* one of the following conditions existed at any time within the preceding twelve months:

(a) There are no persons of that racial group holding those posts.

(b) The proportion of persons of that racial group holding those posts is smaller than the proportion of persons of that racial group employed. For example, if forty per cent of workers in a factory are Asians but only five per cent of the supervisors are Asians, then the proportion of Asians who are supervisors is smaller than the proportion of Asians employed as a whole.

(c) The proportion of persons of that racial group holding those posts is smaller than the proportion of persons of that racial group among the population in the area from which the workforce is normally recruited. This would apply, for instance, where a department store in a predominantly black area had hardly any black sales assistants.

Although employers can discriminate positively by providing special training courses for certain racial groups, or by encouraging them to apply for certain work, they cannot discriminate positively by recruiting or promoting members of that racial group in preference to others.

(d) The discrimination is to comply with laws passed by Parliament or conditions imposed by Ministers (see page 106).

(e) The discrimination is for the purpose of safeguarding national security (see page 107).

Is race discrimination against civil servants unlawful?

Yes, it is. If you apply for a job with, or work for, a Ministry, a government department or a statutory body, race discrimination against you is unlawful in exactly the same way as it is in relation to employment by a private employer. A statutory body is simply one that is created by an Act of Parliament. For example, the Commission for Racial Equality is a statutory body.

There are, however, two exceptions to this. First, you cannot complain of race discrimination if it relates to the holding of a statutory office. A statutory office is one that is created by an Act of Parliament. Lay magistrates and adjudicators who hear immigration appeals are holders of statutory offices. If you feel that you have been discriminated against by not being appointed an adjudicator, you cannot complain about it in law.

Secondly, the Crown and certain specified public bodies are allowed to discriminate in recruitment on the basis of your birth, nationality, descent, or length of residence in this country. Thus, a requirement for a Ministry of Defence job that you and your parents must be British nationals would be lawful in spite of its discriminatory effect. Public bodies allowed to discriminate in this way include the Bank of England, the British Council, the Civil Aviation Authority, the National Audit Office, the National Gallery, the Tate Gallery, the UK Atomic Energy Authority and the Victoria and Albert Museum.

Is race discrimination in the armed forces unlawful?

Yes, it is. The only exception is that discrimination in recruitment is permitted if it is on the basis of your birth, nationality, descent or length of residence in this country. Otherwise, race discrimination is unlawful in the same ways as it is in employment by a private employer. The only difference is that you do not bring your complaint in an industrial tribunal, as you do in other employment cases, but take it up through special internal procedures within the armed forces.

Is race discrimination in the police force unlawful?

For the purposes of race discrimination, policemen and police cadets are employees and it is unlawful for the force to discriminate against them in the same ways as it is for employers to discriminate against employees and potential employees. If you are a cadet or a policeman or policewoman, your employer is either the chief officer of police or the police authority, depending on which of the two has discriminated against you.

24

Proceedings for race discrimination within the police force are brought in an industrial tribunal just as in any other employment case.

What can I do if I have been discriminated against by an employer?

Proceedings for race discrimination by employers are brought in industrial tribunals. Chapter 4 explains how to bring proceedings in an industrial tribunal and the bodies which can provide you with assistance to do so. It is important to remember that proceedings must be started within three months of the act of discrimination taking place. So if you feel that you have been the victim of discrimination, don't waste any time – seek advice immediately.

3: Discrimination in Other Fields of Employment

Is race discrimination unlawful in other areas of employment?

Yes. Race discrimination is unlawful in a wide variety of areas related to your working life. It is unlawful for the following to discriminate racially against you: qualifying bodies (see pages 26–7); training bodies (see pages 27–8); employment agencies and anyone else providing careers guidance (see pages 28–30); trade unions (see pages 30–31); professional and trade organizations (see pages 31–2); and partnerships (see pages 32–3).

What is a 'qualifying body'?

This simply means any authority or body which has it in its power to grant you a qualification or a licence that is either necessary or helpful for engaging in a particular profession or trade. The following are examples of qualifying bodies: the Law Society, which issues practising certificates you must have before you can practise as a solicitor; the Council of Legal Education, which is responsible for the education and examination of those wishing to practise as barristers; and the licensing justices, who grant licences to sell intoxicating liquor either at restaurants or in shops.

What is unlawful discrimination by a qualifying body?

A qualifying body acts unlawfully if it racially discriminates against you by not granting your application for the qualification or licence, by withdrawing it from you if you already have it, or by offering to grant it to you on less favourable terms than it does to other people. For example, a qualifying body has a rule that persons with overseas degrees must do a two-year course in order to obtain the relevant qualification. Those however, with degrees from a UK university only have to do a one-year course in order to obtain the same qualification. This amounts to indirect discrimination by the body in question – unless of course, it can show the requirement to be justifiable.

In some cases there is a right of appeal from the decision of a qualifying body. If such a right exists, you must use it. For instance, you can appeal against a decision of the licensing justices to the Crown Court, and this is the course you must take if you are not satisfied with their decision. If there is no right of appeal, you can bring proceedings for race discrimination in an industrial tribunal.

What is a 'training body'?
For the purposes of race discrimination the following are classified as 'training bodies':

(a) Industrial training boards established by the Minister of Labour in order to provide training for jobs in commerce and industry to persons over compulsory school age.

(b) The Manpower Services Commission.

(c) Any association of employers which has as its principal object, or as one of its principal objects, giving its employees access to training facilities.

(d) Any person who agrees with the Manpower Services Commission to take on trainees under the Training Opportunities Scheme or the Youth Training Scheme. This covers the situation where employers act as sponsors and take on trainees to work for them under

27

either scheme. A sponsor who discriminates against a trainee does so not as an employer (there is no contract of employment involved) but as a 'training body'.

What is unlawful discrimination by training bodies?

A training body acts unlawfully if it racially discriminates against you by not providing you with training facilities, or by terminating your training, or by giving you access to training facilities on less favourable terms than to others. For example, industrial training boards may pay maintenance and travelling expenses to individuals attending courses provided by them. If such payments are made to white persons attending a course but not to black persons doing so, that is unlawful race discrimination by the board. Similarly, an employer who refuses to take black trainees under the Youth Training Scheme is discriminating unlawfully.

Industrial training boards and the Manpower Services Commission are, however, entitled to discriminate positively in certain circumstances. They can only do so if they believe that a particular racial group is unrepresented or under-represented in a particular sphere of work. (This position might exist in the country as a whole or only in particular areas.) If this is the case, or has been the case at any time within the previous twelve months, they can discriminate positively either in the provision of training facilities or by encouraging persons of the racial group in question to take advantage of opportunities for doing that work.

What is an 'employment agency'?

The term 'employment agency' refers to any person who provides services (and that includes guidance on careers) for the purpose of finding jobs for workers or supplying employers with workers. It is irrelevant whether such services are provided free or for financial gain. The term 'employment agency' includes job centres, Careers Service offices, and heads of careers at schools.

What is unlawful discrimination by an employment agency?

An employment agency acts unlawfully if it discriminates racially against you either by not providing you with any of its services or by treating you less favourably in the provision of its services. The following are examples of unlawful discrimination by employment agencies:

An employer instructs an agency that Asian applicants are not wanted. Although the agency has a number of Asians on its books who are suitable candidates for the job in question, it does not send any of them for an interview.

The head of careers at a girls' school distinguishes between black and white pupils when providing guidance on careers. The white girls are advised and encouraged to go to universities and enter the professions. Black girls, on the other hand, are encouraged to take sales and catering jobs upon leaving school. The advice is not in any way related to the girls' academic abilities.

An employment agency, however, does not break the law if it discriminates against you in relation to a job which the employer could lawfully refuse to offer you (see pages 19–23). For example, a Jewish family instructs an agency to send them a nanny but stipulates that it does not want an Arab. The agency has a suitable Arab nanny on their books but does not send her for an interview. As the employment is for the purposes of a private household, the family could lawfully refuse to hire an Arab nanny. Thus there is no unlawful discrimination by the agency.

An agency is also not liable for discrimination if it can prove that it reasonably relied on a statement made by the employer that he or she could lawfully refuse to offer the person in question the relevant job. If employers knowingly or recklessly make a false statement to this effect, they can be prosecuted in a magistrates' court and could be fined if convicted.

What is unlawful discrimination by trade unions?

It is unlawful for a trade union to discriminate racially against people wishing to join, either by not offering them membership or by being prepared to accept them on less favourable terms than other members. If a union's admission rules are discriminatory, then that in itself can be the basis for a claim of racial discrimination.

If you are already a member of a union, it must not discriminate against you by depriving you of that membership or by treating you less favourably with regard to the benefits, facilities and services it provides. These may include training facilities, welfare and insurance schemes, entertainment and social events, processing of grievances, and negotiations and assistance in disciplinary or dismissal procedures.

Officials of unions, such as shop stewards, are not personally liable if they discriminate racially against particular members. If, however, they do anything discriminatory with the authority of the union, then the union is liable for their acts.

It is also unlawful for trade union members or representatives to persuade or induce, or to try to persuade or induce, an employer to discriminate racially in the recruitment, promotion, transfer, training or dismissal of employees. This, however, is something in respect of which only the Commission for Racial Equality can take action (see page 114).

Are trade unions allowed to discriminate positively?

Positive discrimination is allowed only in the following two areas:

(a) To provide training only for members of a particular racial group for certain union posts, or to encourage only members of that racial group to take up those posts. A union can only take this positive measure if at any time within the previous twelve months there has been no person of the racial group in question holding that particular post, or the proportion of people of that racial group holding that post was small compared to the proportion of people of that group in the union. For example, twenty per cent of a union's members are Asians. However, only two per cent of the branch secretaries are Asians. In these circumstances, the union would be acting lawfully if it provided training for, or encouraged, only Asians to become branch secretaries. However, it would not be acting lawfully if it positively discriminated in favour of Asians in *selecting* its branch secretaries.

(b) To encourage only persons of a particular racial group to join the union where at any time in the previous twelve months there were either no members from that racial group, or the proportion of members from that racial group was small in comparison with the proportion of persons of that racial group who were eligible for membership.

What are professional and trade organizations?

A professional organization is one whose members carry out a particular profession, occupation or vocation for the purposes of which the organization exists. This includes such bodies as the Bar Council, the Law Society, the British Medical Association, the Royal Institute of British Architects, and the British Association of Social Workers. A trade organization is one whose members carry out a particular trade or business for the purposes of which the organization exists.

Is race discrimination by professional and trade organizations unlawful?

It is unlawful for a professional or a trade organization to discriminate racially against existing and potential members. It must not racially discriminate against potential members, either by not accepting their applications or by being prepared to accept them on less favourable terms than other members.

If you are already a member of such an organization it must not racially discriminate against you either by taking your membership away or by treating you less favourably in any way, especially in relation to the benefits, facilities and services it provides.

Professional and trade organizations are entitled to discriminate positively by encouraging persons of a particular racial group to join, or by training persons of a particular racial group for certain posts in the organization and by encouraging them to take up those posts. The circumstances in which they can do this are the same as those in which trade unions can discriminate positively (see page 31).

Is it unlawful for a firm to discriminate against partners?

Yes, but only if the firm has six or more partners. Most professionals such as doctors, dentists, solicitors, accountants, surveyors and architects operate as partnerships. The majority of these, however, are small firms or practices, and normally consist of less than six partners.

Not only is it unlawful for existing firms to discriminate, but also for individuals proposing to form themselves into a partnership – provided, of course, that the firm will consist of six or more partners.

If you apply to join a firm of six or more partners, it is unlawful for the firm to use a discriminatory selection procedure, or to discriminate against you either by not accepting you as a partner or by offering to do so on less favourable terms than the other partners.

If you are already a partner in a firm of six or more partners, it must not racially discriminate against you in relation to any of its benefits, facilities or services or in expelling you from that position.

What can I do if I am discriminated against by any of the above?

You can bring proceedings for race discrimination in an industrial tribunal (see Chapter 4).

4: Proceedings in the Industrial Tribunal

Where do I bring proceedings for race discrimination in the employment field?
All proceedings for race discrimination relating to employment (as explained in Chapters 2 and 3) are brought in an industrial tribunal, except if they relate to the armed forces (see page 24) or to a qualifying body (see page 27).

Every application should initially be sent to the Central Office of Industrial Tribunals (COIT), of which there are three.

For England and Wales:
  93 Ebury Bridge Road,
  London SW1 (telephone: 01-730 9161).

For Scotland:
  St Andrew's House,
  141 West Nile Street,
  Glasgow G1 2RU (telephone: 041-331 1601).

For Northern Ireland:
  Bedford House,
  16–22 Bedford Street,
  Belfast BT2 7NR (telephone: 0232-327666).

The person to whom applications must be sent is the Secretary of the Tribunals.

Once an application has been registered at the COIT, the Secretary then delegates it to the relevant Regional Office of Industrial Tribunals, which thereafter has charge of it. Regional offices have been established at Ashford, Birmingham, Bristol, Bury St Edmunds, Cardiff, Exeter, Leeds, London, Liverpool, Manchester, Newcastle-upon-Tyne, Nottingham, Sheffield and Southampton. Within each region, there are certain centres where hearings take place.

At the hearing, the tribunal will consist of three people: a chairperson, who will be either a solicitor or a barrister of at least seven years' standing, and two non-lawyers. One of the two will have been appointed after consultation with employers' organizations and the other after consultation with trade unions. All three are equal members and they all participate in deciding the case, although the written decision will be signed only by the chairperson. The decision of the tribunal can be either unanimous or that of a majority.

Unfortunately, there is no requirement to have a black person sitting on the tribunal when deciding race discrimination cases. The tribunal should simply try to ensure that at least one of the lay members has special knowledge of race relations.

A tribunal can proceed with a case if it consists of the chairperson and only one lay member, so long as both parties agree to it. If both parties do not agree, the hearing will have to be adjourned.

Each tribunal also has a clerk who is not a legally qualified person. The clerk will normally approach you before the hearing and explain the procedure and ask you for the names of your witnesses. He or she will be present throughout the hearing and at the end will advise you as to how you and your witnesses can claim expenses. Expenses which are allowed are loss of wages, travelling expenses and any other expenditure which you have incurred as a result of having to attend the hearing.

How do I start proceedings?

Proceedings before an industrial tribunal are started by sending an application to the Secretary of Tribunals at the relevant COIT (for the addresses, see page 34).

There is a standard application form known as the 'IT1' for starting proceedings. This form is available from the COIT, Regional Offices of the Industrial Tribunals, employment exchanges and law centres. Although it is not essential to use this particular form, you should try and use it if you can obtain one.

If you cannot get hold of the form 'IT1' you can start proceedings simply by writing a letter to the Secretary of Tribunals at the COIT, stating your name and address, the name and address of the person about whom you are complaining and the grounds on which you claim to have been discriminated.

Although this appears to be simple enough, you should try and get legal advice before presenting your application. In some cases you may be entitled to claim for sex discrimination and/or unfair dismissal, in addition to claiming for race discrimination. It is important to try and make sure that you start proceedings against the right person. For example, although you work for a subsidiary company, your real employer may be the parent company.

Are there any time limits within which I must start proceedings?

An industrial tribunal will not consider your complaint unless your application is received at the COIT within three months of the act of discrimination taking place. In calculating when the three-month period expires, you must include the date on which the act of discrimination took place and remember that a month means an ordinary calendar month.

Thus, if you are discriminated against on 6 February your application must be received by midnight on 5 May.

Where the discrimination relates to a dismissal, the date from which the three-month period is calculated is not the date when the notice of dismissal was given but the date on which the notice expires and your job effectively comes to an end.

Even if the person about whom you are complaining does not take the point that your application was presented out of time, the tribunal itself may do so and refuse to hear your complaint.

The important thing is that your application must be delivered at the COIT office within the three-month period. It does not necessarily have to be handed over to anybody there. Thus, if the last day of your time limit falls on a Saturday, your application will have been presented in time if you push it through the letterbox of the COIT on that day. If the last day is a Saturday or a Sunday and it is at all possible for you to deliver it at the COIT on that day, do so – do not wait until the Monday.

Don't rely on the postal service and post your application the day before the three-month time limit expires. Even with a first-class stamp, there is no guarantee that it will reach the COIT the following day.

If, however, you post your application three or four days in advance of the expiry date, but it is nevertheless delayed and arrives after the expiry date, the tribunal will determine as a preliminary issue whether it was in fact posted on the day that you say. If they come to the conclusion that it was, they will consider your application.

Are there any circumstances in which the industrial tribunal will extend the time limit?

A tribunal will hear your complaint, although it is out of time, if it considers that in all the circumstances of the case it would be 'just and equitable' to do so. The tribunal at this stage will not be concerned with the merits of your case (that is, whether you have a strong or a weak case) but with your reasons for not presenting your application in time.

In such a situation the tribunal will consider your knowledge, belief, experience and all the relevant circumstances. In some cases, the time limit may be extended because you did not know about your rights or the time limit. However, if you had legal advice or access to legal advice, it is very unlikely that this will suffice. The decision in each case will depend on the individual concerned and the relevant facts.

If you are pursuing an appeal under the internal disputes procedure at your place of work, don't wait for the outcome of that before starting proceedings. Start proceedings within the three-month period.

What if I suspect that I have been discriminated against, but I need further information?

If you think you have been discriminated against, or know that you have but require further information in order to prepare your case, you can send the discriminator a form asking certain questions. A standard form known as the 'Questionnaire of person aggrieved' is obtainable free of charge from the Commission for Racial Equality (CRE), any local employment centre or job centre, or any Community Relations Council.

On this form you state your name and address and relate the facts which you think amount to discrimination. You then ask the person to whom it is sent whether he or she agrees with your version of events and, if not, in what respect they disagree with it. You then ask whether they accept that their treatment of you was unlawful discrimination and, if not, ask their reasons for it and the extent to which consideration of colour or race affected it. You may then ask any other questions which you think are relevant. For example, if you think that you were not offered a job because you are black, you can ask how many people applied for the job, how many of them were white, how many black, how many were interviewed or shortlisted and what their colour was, the colour of the successful applicant, the criteria used for selecting someone, how you fell short of the criteria, etc.

The questions you ask and the replies you are given can be used as evidence in your case provided that they are served either before you present your application to the industrial tribunal or within twenty-one days of your doing so. If you wish to serve it any later and use it as evidence, you will need the leave of the tribunal to do so.

If the discriminator does not reply to your questions, or gives answers which appear to be vague or evasive, the tribunal may draw from that whatever inference it wishes. It may well infer that the person concerned has discriminated unlawfully.

Another reason why it is useful to serve this form is that once discriminators have given certain reasons for their behaviour, they are stuck with them. If they give a different version or different reasons at the hearing, then this will cast a doubt on their truthfulness and may well lead to the conclusion that they are lying because they have discriminated unlawfully.

Can I get any help with my case and, if so, will I have to pay for it?

The first thing to remember is that legal aid is not available for proceedings in an industrial tribunal. There are, however, organizations and persons who can help you either by giving you advice or by preparing your case and representing you at the hearing without your having to pay for it.

The Commission for Racial Equality
  Elliot House,
  10–12 Allington Street,
  London SW1 (telephone: 01-828 7022).

The CRE can provide you with assistance (free of charge) in a variety of circumstances. If you want them to help you, apply in writing, setting out as much detail as you can about the act of discrimination. Before reaching any decision, the CRE will usually send out a questionnaire to the discriminator in order to get more information. Usually, the CRE will write to you within two months of receiving your application, informing you whether they have decided to assist you or not. In some cases, they may write to you within the two-month period, stating that they need another month in order to reach a decision.

The CRE will agree to assist you if your case raises a question of principle and is likely to have wider effects than determining just your individual case. They will also provide assistance if they think that it is unreal for you to deal with the case without any help, either because it is a complex case or because of your position in relation to that of the discriminator. This would apply, for instance, where the discriminator is a rich and powerful organization and you are an individual without any resources. Finally, the CRE has a wide discretion to assist you if they feel that there is some special

consideration in your case which merits it. In 1985 the
CRE received 734 applications for assistance in the
employment field. They provided assistance in only
138 cases.

If the CRE decides to assist you, they can do so in a
variety of ways. They may simply give you advice.
Alternatively they may take on your case, with one of
their employees (who will be a qualified lawyer) acting
on your behalf. This person will prepare the case and
represent you at the hearing. They may send your case
to a solicitor, who will then take over its conduct. The
solicitor may deal with it personally or may engage a
barrister. In any case, you will be legally represented at
the hearing.

If the CRE agrees to assist you, it won't cost you a
penny and you will get qualified lawyers taking on your
case. The only problem is that it takes them quite some
time to reach a decision and you may suddenly be told
at the eleventh hour that you are not getting any help.

Free Representation Unit (FRU)
3 Middle Temple Lane,
London EC4 (telephone: 01-353 3697).

FRU does not take on cases directly, but receives re-
ferrals from Citizens' Advice Bureaux and law centres.
If your case is referred at an early stage, FRU will help
you prepare it and advise you on settling it. If it is
received at a later stage, FRU will provide someone
to represent you at the tribunal. In either event, it won't
cost you anything. The person who will represent you
will be a barrister or a solicitor, or someone training to
be a barrister or a solicitor, or a law student. Although
they may not be a qualified lawyer, they will probably
have had some experience of industrial tribunal cases.
As FRU relies on lawyers volunteering their services,
it cannot always guarantee representation but does

provide it in about seventy per cent of the cases referred to it.

Trade unions

If you belong to a trade union, your shop steward or union official may be able to help you bring your case and represent you at the hearing.

Law centres

Find out if there is a law centre in your area (look under 'Law Centres' in the phone directory, or phone the Law Centres Federation on 01-387 8570) and go and see them. They will be able to provide you with free advice, assistance and representation for your case.

Citizens' Advice Bureaux

Find the nearest Citizens' Advice Bureau to you (look in the phone directory under 'Citizens' Advice Bureaux'). It is advisable to call first, as they do not always open during normal working hours. They will be able to advise you on the merits of your case and how to start proceedings. They will also be able to refer you to other organizations which could provide you with assistance and representation.

Solicitors

Solicitors can provide free, or partly free, advice under something known as the 'green form' scheme. Under this, the solicitor can advise you on the merits of your case, help you in filling out your originating application and advise you as to the evidence you will need to back up your claim. However, the solicitor is not covered by this scheme to represent you at the tribunal and, therefore, cannot provide you with free representation. If he or she appears for you at the tribunal and conducts your case for you, you will be charged for it.

What if the discriminator refuses to allow me to see documents which are relevant to the case?

A discriminator does not have to show you any documents unless you obtain a formal order for discovery from the industrial tribunal. You can apply for this either before the hearing by giving notice of it to the Secretary of the Tribunals or at the hearing itself. The tribunal can then order the discriminator to give you copies of the relevant documents or allow you to inspect them, and they will impose a time limit by which the order is to be complied with.

The tribunal may order 'discovery' of documents which are or have been in the discriminator's possession and relate to any question in the proceedings. The criterion used in deciding to make such an order is whether it is necessary for disposing fairly of the proceedings or for saving costs.

If the documents you want to look at contain confidential information or relate to people who are not directly involved in the proceedings, the tribunal can still allow you to see them, but may take steps to cover up or black out names and certain other matters. For example, you complain of discrimination because you were not offered a certain job and you want to see the application forms of the other applicants. The tribunal will probably order that the names and addresses of the other applicants not be disclosed, but that you are entitled to see details of their qualifications and experience.

If the discriminator does not comply with an order for 'discovery', the tribunal may strike out in whole or in part the notice of appearance (the document containing the discriminator's defence to your allegations) and, where appropriate, may even stop the discriminator from opposing your application altogether. However, this can only be done if, after the time limit for complying with the order has expired, the tribunal sends the discriminator a notice and gives him/her every opportunity to say why such a course should not be adopted.

Do conciliation officers become involved at all?

Once you present your application to the industrial tribunal, the Secretary will send copies of all the relevant papers to a conciliation officer. The officer then usually contacts both sides (you and the discriminator) to offer his or her services. If both parties want this help, or if the conciliation officer feels able to act with a reasonable prospect of success, then it is his or her duty to try to resolve the matter without it having to go to the industrial tribunal. If you wish, you can ask for the assistance of a conciliation officer before presenting your claim.

If you are still in employment and have not yet started proceedings, the conciliation officer will usually encourage you to use any internal procedures that are available at your place of work. If you decide to follow this course, keep in mind the date by which you must start proceedings (see page 38).

Anything that is said or written to a conciliation officer in connection with the performance of their duties cannot be used as evidence at the hearing without the agreement of the person who wrote or said it.

If a conciliation officer becomes involved, they will take a neutral stand and their role will simply be to help you and the discriminator reach some kind of an agreement.

Where a settlement is reached with the help of a conciliation officer, it will usually contain an agreement not to pursue the matter in an industrial tribunal. Once you have accepted the settlement, you cannot start or continue with proceedings in the industrial tribunal in respect of the same matter. It will usually contain a denial of any discrimination by the discriminator, even though he/she has agreed to pay you a certain sum of money.

In what circumstances should I settle a case?

'Settling a case' means accepting the sum of money offered to you by the discriminator and not pursuing your case in the industrial tribunal. This can happen at any stage before the hearing starts at the tribunal. A settlement is an agreement between the two parties concerned and usually involves a joint statement signed by both of them or their representatives. The discriminator will never accept that he/she has discriminated, and may wish specifically to deny having discriminated, even though they are offering you money.

Before deciding whether or not to accept a settlement, take legal advice as to the strength of your case and the amount of damages that a tribunal is likely to award you (for damages, see page 52). If you do not have a very strong case and you think that you may have difficulty in proving discrimination, it is advisable to accept a settlement. But remember that you do not have to accept the figure that the discriminator has mentioned; you can negotiate. The better your case, the stronger your bargaining position. If you have a very strong case, the discriminator may be willing to offer you more than a tribunal would. Push for as high a sum as you can. In such cases, discriminators are often more concerned about the adverse publicity that a finding of discrimination would bring than about the money they have to give you.

The discriminator may try to make you formally accept that there was no discrimination and that the details of the settlement should not be made public. In most cases, it would be better not to accept either of those terms.

In some cases you may still be in the job where the discrimination took place. If that is the case, try to make sure the settlement includes an undertaking by your employer not to victimize you for bringing proceedings for race discrimination. It would, of course, be illegal for the employer to do so, but having an undertaking to that effect emphasizes the point. Try also to get your employer to agree to adopt an equal opportunity policy in consultation with your union.

If your employer accepts that discrimination took place, demand an apology and an undertaking that no discrimination will take place in the future. If the discrimination was in the form of racial abuse in the course of your employment, ask that it be made a disciplinary offence.

There are various other terms that can be incorporated into a settlement. The terms on which you settle your case will depend on the facts of your case. It is important, however, that you remember that getting a good deal for yourself should not be the only consideration; try to ensure, as far as is possible, that other persons will not suffer the same discrimination that you did.

How do I prepare for the hearing?

You will be given at least fourteen days' notice of the place and date of the hearing. Make sure that anyone who can support your account is available to give evidence on the day of the hearing. If any of your witnesses is not available, take a signed, written statement from them. This can be used in evidence although it will not carry the same weight as the witness giving evidence in person. If you intend to rely on a written statement, you must send copies of it at least seven days before the hearing to the Secretary of the Tribunals and to the other side. If the unavailable witness is very important to your case, try writing to the Secretary well in advance to ask if your hearing can be moved to another date.

The other important thing is the documents to which you intend to refer in the course of the hearing. These may include a newspaper advertisement, your application for a job, your contract of employment, a letter from the employer dismissing you, a certificate of your qualifications, etc. Make photocopies of all the relevant documents – including your originating application, the other side's notice of appearance, a questionnaire (if any was sent) and the answer to it – and clip them all together. Number the documents and make an index listing the documents and the pages at which they are to be found. This is your 'bundle'. Make sure that you have six copies of the bundle. Send one to the other side before the hearing; they may wish to add nothing to it, in which case it becomes an 'agreed bundle', or they may prefer to prepare a bundle of their own. Three copies will be required for the tribunal; these may be handed to the clerk on the day of the hearing. One will be your copy, and the last one can be used by witnesses when giving evidence.

What is the procedure at the hearing?

Proceedings in an industrial tribunal are, on the whole, less formal than in a court of law. You can either appear yourself or be represented by a solicitor, a barrister, a representative of your trade union or anyone else that you want.

As it is up to you to prove discrimination, you or your representative will open the case and call your evidence first. 'Opening a case' simply means giving a brief outline of your case with reference to the documents in your bundle. Then you give your evidence and call any witnesses who support your case. It is entirely a matter for you to decide in what order you call your witnesses, and it is your duty to ensure that all the relevant evidence is before the tribunal. The other side will cross-examine your witnesses, and in doing so will put to them the facts on which they rely. Once you have called all your evidence, it will be the turn of the other side to call their witnesses, and you will be entitled to cross-examine them. At the end of the evidence, both sides will have an opportunity to sum up their respective cases.

If you are not represented, the tribunal will explain to you the procedure and the relevant law and will generally help you to present your case. However, they will not tell you what evidence to call, nor will they cross-examine the other side's witnesses for you. As far as your evidence is concerned, they will either allow you to give your account without being interrupted or will ask you questions and treat your answers as your evidence.

At the end of the hearing, the tribunal may give you their decision there and then, or they may decide later on. In any event, they will send you their decision in writing and their reasons for reaching that decision.

How do I prove direct discrimination?
You will have to prove to the tribunal, first, that you were treated less favourably than others and, second, that it is more likely than not that the reason for it was your race, colour, etc. It is extremely difficult to find hard concrete evidence of race discrimination. A person who discriminates against you on racial grounds is hardly likely to put that forward as a way of explaining their behaviour.

Tribunals are well aware of the difficulties of proving

race discrimination and, therefore, adopt the following approach when determining cases. Once a tribunal is satisfied that you were treated less favourably, it will then look carefully at the reasons given for it by the discriminator. For example, if you, a black person, prove that a white person less qualified and suitable than you was promoted instead of you, or that a vacancy was still being advertised after the employer had seen you and told you that it was filled, you have proved that you were treated less favourably. The employer must then provide an explanation. In the absence of any explanation, or of a satisfactory and credible explanation, the tribunal is entitled to conclude that you were unlawfully discriminated against on racial grounds. The fact that the employer denies that race had anything to do with his/her behaviour is not in itself enough. Clear and concise reasons have to be given for such behaviour. If the tribunal accept these reasons as genuine, your claim will be dismissed. If not, you will succeed.

If the discriminator has deliberately and without reasonable excuse failed to reply to the questionnaire sent by you (see page 38), or has answered it vaguely or evasively, the tribunal may infer from that that he/she has unlawfully discriminated against you.

You can rely on acts of discrimination in the past in respect of which no proceedings were brought and for which the time limit has already expired in order to show that the act about which you are complaining was race discrimination. For example, you are black and in July 1986 your application for promotion is turned down although you are a suitable candidate. A white person with fewer qualifications and less experience than you is promoted instead. You can bring evidence to show that the same thing happened in July 1985, and rely on it to show that you were discriminated against in July 1986.

You can also produce evidence about things which happened *after* the act about which you are complaining, in order to show that that act was discriminatory. For instance, in the above example, you could produce evidence to show that the person responsible for deciding who should be promoted said to someone else in August or September 1986 that blacks were all right in clerical posts but not up to the standard for anything higher. The purpose of bringing in that evidence would be to show that this person was motivated by racial considerations in deciding not to promote you. The person would then have to explain the racist remarks.

If you are a West Indian and allege race discrimination against a large company because they refused to offer you a job, the mere fact that the company employs other workers from ethnic minorities is not in itself enough to show that they did not discriminate against you. It depends to a large extent on the numbers and ethnic origins of the black workers employed by them, and on the positions in which they are employed. If there are only three black workers and they are all Asians, that does not particularly help the company in denying your allegations. Even if one of their employees is a West Indian, that again is not enough bearing in mind the size of the company. If the employment of one West Indian was enough to rebut the allegation of discrimination, every large company could employ the token one and then happily discriminate against the rest.

How do I prove indirect discrimination?
In order to prove indirect discrimination you have to prove three things. First, that the discriminator has imposed a particular requirement or condition. Second, that you cannot comply with it and, third, that the

proportion of your racial group who can comply with it is considerably smaller than the proportion of other racial groups who can comply with it (see pages 2–5).

Proving the first two elements is quite straightforward and should not pose any problems. The other side will normally accept that the relevant requirement or condition was imposed and that you could not comply with it. Proving the third element can be more difficult. In some cases it may be self-evident and not require statistical evidence. For example, if a condition of 'no beards' or 'no turbans' is imposed, the tribunal and the other side will probably accept, without any statistical evidence being produced, that the proportion of Sikhs who could comply with it would be smaller than the proportion of non-Sikhs who could comply with it. In other cases, statistical evidence will be required – as, for example, when it is alleged that an age requirement has a disproportionately adverse effect on a particular racial group, or that a requirement as to residence in a particular area is discriminatory.

In some cases it may be difficult to produce wholly comprehensive statistical evidence. The tribunal may then accept statistical evidence based on a sample, especially if the other side has not produced any evidence to counter it, and there has been no suggestion that your evidence gives a distorted or inaccurate picture.

Once you have proved these three elements, it is then for the discriminator to show that the condition or requirement was justifiable (see page 4). If this cannot be done, you will succeed in your claim.

What can the tribunal do if I prove discrimination?

Once the tribunal is satisfied that you were discriminated against, they may do one of the following two things.

First, they may recommend that the discriminator takes certain action within a specified period for the purpose of removing or reducing the adverse effect which the discrimination had on you. Thus if a tribunal finds that you were not promoted to a particular position because of race discrimination, they may recommend that you be promoted to that position as soon as there is a vacancy for it. They can only make a recommendation which relates to you personally; they cannot make a general recommendation in order to improve race relations or to ensure that others will not suffer the same discrimination as you. If the discriminator does not follow the tribunal's recommendation, the tribunal may award you money if none has been awarded so far or it may increase the sum originally awarded.

Second, the tribunal can award you a sum of money. The amount of money awarded will depend upon the circumstances of your particular case and the loss, if any, which you have suffered. There are three particular matters in respect of which the tribunal can award you money:

Injury to feelings
This is money given to you for the offence and distress caused to you by the act of discrimination. It varies according to the circumstances in which the discrimination took place, but is usually in the region of £200–300.

Loss of Job Opportunity
This is generally awarded when you are not offered a job because of race discrimination. Whether any money is awarded – and the amount which is given – depends on a number of factors: your qualifications and experience, the type of job applied for, the general avail-

ability of jobs of that kind and how certain it was that you would have got the job had it not been for the discrimination. The more scarce and specialized the job, the higher the award of damages. For example, if you are not offered the position of consultant neuro-surgeon, the damages will be considerable. If, on the other hand, the job in question is a clerical job and one which requires no qualification or special skills, you will get hardly any money for loss of job opportunity.

Loss of Earnings

This is normally awarded where the discrimination relates to a dismissal and is intended to compensate you for the financial loss caused by the dismissal. In calculating your loss you use as the starting point your net pay, that is, what you used to receive after tax and national insurance deductions. You also include and take into account regular overtime which you did, any bonus payments and fringe benefits.

Remember that it is your duty to act reasonably after your dismissal and to do whatever you can to decrease your loss. Thus you should make every effort to find another job. Keep a record of your efforts to do so and also copies of any relevant documents (advertisements which you answered, job applications, letters from employers, etc.). The tribunal would probably consider it unreasonable for you to refuse another similar job simply because it does not pay as well as your old one. If the tribunal feels that you did not make any effort to find another job, or that you unreasonably refused to accept one that was offered, they will reduce the amount of money awarded to you.

In deciding the amount of money to give you for loss of earnings, the tribunal will first calculate the loss of earnings between the date of dismissal and the date of hearing and, second, the future loss of earnings.

The first is relatively easy to work out – it is the net amount you would have earned in your old job minus the amount you have actually earned in your new job, or should have earned had you taken steps to reduce your loss. If you earn more in your new job, the extra earnings in the new job will be set off against your loss.

The second is more difficult to work out and involves guesswork to a large extent. If by the time of the hearing you have a new job and it pays less than your old one, the future loss of earnings will be the difference between the two net wages for a specified period of time in the future. If the new job pays more than the old, then there is no future loss of earnings.

If you do not have a new job by the date of the hearing, it becomes more complicated. In assessing how much to award, the tribunal will take into account such matters as when you are likely to get a new job and how much you are likely to earn in that job. This depends, of course, on your qualifications and skills and the local employment situation.

The maximum amount of money the tribunal can give you is £8,000. If you claim for sex discrimination and/or unfair dismissal as well, the maximum you can get in respect of everything is still £8,000.

If your complaint was about indirect discrimination and the tribunal find that it is proved, they cannot award you any money if the discriminator proves that the requirement or condition in question was not applied with the *intention* of racially discriminating against you.

Will I have to pay the other side's costs if I lose?
Not usually. It is only in exceptional circumstances that the tribunal will ask you to pay the other side's costs. It will only do so if in bringing or conducting your case you have acted 'frivolously', 'vexatiously' or otherwise

unreasonably. You will have acted 'frivolously' if you brought your claim knowing that there was no substance in it and it was bound to fail. You will have acted 'vexatiously' if you brought a hopeless claim, not because you thought you might win but out of spite to harass someone or for some other improper motive.

In deciding whether you should be ordered to pay the other side's costs, the tribunal will take into account your ability, or lack of it, to meet such an order. If an order is made against you, it will usually be for a fixed sum.

The only other instance in which you may be ordered to pay the other side's costs is if the hearing has to be adjourned because of you. Whether you are so ordered will depend on the reasons for the adjournment. If, for example, you apply at the hearing to amend your application by adding new details to it, and the other side asks for an adjournment because it needs time to consider the new allegations, then you will have to pay the other side's costs for attending on that day. If, however, the adjournment is due to something completely unforeseen and not in any way your fault, then you won't have to pay the other side's costs (for example, if you fall ill and are taken to hospital the night before the hearing).

If you are assisted by the Commission for Racial Equality (CRE) and are ordered to pay costs, the CRE will do so on your behalf.

If you win the case and the tribunal is of the opinion that the discriminator has acted frivolously, vexatiously or otherwise unreasonably in defending the case, they can order him or her to pay your legal costs if you have incurred any. Similarly, if the case has to be adjourned because of the discriminator doing something at a late stage, the discriminator will have to pay your legal costs for attending on that day.

Can I appeal if I lose my case?

Yes, but only if you can show one or more of the following:

(a) That the tribunal misdirected itself in law, or misunderstood the law, or misapplied the law.

(b) That the tribunal misunderstood or misapplied the facts.

(c) That the decision of the tribunal was perverse or that there was no evidence to justify the conclusion which was reached. In order to show that a decision was perverse you would have to show that no tribunal, having applied the law correctly, could have reached that decision. It is not enough to show that the tribunal relied on evidence which was hard to believe.

You appeal from an industrial tribunal to the Employment Appeal Tribunal. The central office is:

4 St James' Square,

London SW1Y 4JB (telephone: 01-214 3367).

The important thing to remember is that, unlike for a case in the industrial tribunal, you can get legal aid for bringing or defending proceedings in the Employment Appeal Tribunal (EAT). As proceedings in the EAT involve legal arguments, it is better to engage a lawyer than to try and conduct them yourself.

You start the appeal proceedings by sending the EAT a Notice of Appeal and a copy of the written reasons for the industrial tribunal's decision. The time limit for appealing is forty-two days from the day on which the written reasons for the decision were sent to you. If you appeal after the forty-two-day period has expired, your Notice of Appeal must be accompanied by an application for extension of time, setting out the reasons for the delay. You will only be allowed to appeal out of time in exceptional circumstances and it will depend primarily on whether you have a good excuse for the delay. It will not necessarily be a good excuse to say that the reason for the delay is that legal aid was not granted within the forty-two-day period, or that you were trying to get assistance from the CRE, your trade union or some other body.

If, on reading the Notice of Appeal, the EAT feels that there is no arguable point of law, it may set the case for a hearing on a preliminary point. It will then be for the person appealing to show why the appeal should not be dismissed. If they fail, the appeal will be dismissed. If they succeed, the appeal will be set down for a hearing and will be heard at a later date. There will be a similar hearing on a preliminary point if the appeal depends solely or mainly on the grounds that the tribunal took an erroneous view of the evidence or reached an unreasonable conclusion upon the facts. These are fairly short hearings and generally do not take more than an hour.

You will have to send to the EAT only those documents which were before the tribunal *and* are relevant to the appeal. There is no need to send *all* the documents which were used before the tribunal.

At the beginning of each month, the EAT publishes a list of all the cases to be heard in the following month. You will be notified as soon as your case appears on the list. If you cannot attend on the date given to you, you may apply to the listing office to have the date altered, but must do so before the fifteenth of the month in which the case appeared in the list.

At the hearing of the appeal you can appear in person or be represented by lawyers or any other person of your choice.

The person who loses the appeal will not normally have to pay the other side's costs unless the EAT considers that the proceedings were unnecessary, improper or vexatious or that there has been an unreasonable delay or other unreasonable conduct in bringing or conducting the proceedings. The kind of case in which you would normally have to pay costs is where the appeal was not based on any point of law and you abandon it on the day of the hearing or shortly before it.

You can appeal on a question of law from the EAT to the Court of Appeal. In order to do so you have to get the leave of either the EAT or the Court of Appeal. The time limit for appealing to the Court of Appeal is four weeks from the date of the decision of the EAT.

5: Education

In what areas of education is race discrimination unlawful?
There are three aspects of education in which race discrimination is against the law. First, it is unlawful for schools to discriminate against your children. This applies equally to primary and secondary schools, regardless of whether the school in question is a state, independent or special school.

State schools are maintained by local education authorities and provide your children with free education. Each local education authority divides its districts into 'catchment areas' and allots one to each school. Your child will normally go to a school in the catchment area in which you live. Independent schools are private schools (more commonly known as 'public' schools) and you have to pay fees for your child to attend one of them. Special schools are for children who have special needs, such as children who are blind, deaf, educationally subnormal, severely physically handicapped or maladjusted. Some special schools are maintained by local education authorities and are free, others are independent and fee-paying.

Second, it is unlawful for a large number of institutions which provide further education to discriminate against you. Third, a local education authority must not discriminate against you in carrying out any of its functions.

All of these are explained more fully in the rest of this chapter.

What is unlawful discrimination by schools?

If your child is applying to a particular school, it is unlawful for that school to discriminate racially against the child either by not admitting him or her to that school or by offering to do so on less favourable terms than for other pupils.

The refusal to admit a child to a school often takes the form of indirect discrimination; that is, the school imposes a certain requirement or condition with which your child cannot comply because you belong to a particular racial group. For example, the school has a rule that all girls must wear a grey skirt and short white socks, and your daughter is a traditional Muslim who does not want to expose her legs. Unless the school can show the requirement to be justified, it is unlawful race discrimination. Remember, it is no defence for the school to say that the reasons for having a uniform are largely reasons of practical convenience, to minimize external differences between different races and social classes and to discourage competitive fashion among teenagers, or to say that there would be difficulties in enforcing the rules against the other children if the school was seen to be making a concession for your child. Nor is it enough for a Christian school to say that they object to leg-coverings because they are the outward manifestation of a non-Christian faith. (The circumstances in which discrimination may be lawful are described below.)

If your children already attend school, it is unlawful for the school to racially discriminate against them by not allowing them to attend classes or courses or by refusing them access to any other benefits, facilities or services which it provides or by treating them less favourably in any other way. The following are examples of unlawful race discrimination against pupils.

The school has a policy of putting all the Bengali children in each year in the same class. They feel that the Bengali children will be happier and more comfortable with each other. Thus all the Bengalis are in one class, all the whites in another. This is segregation and is unlawful.

The school encourages black children to sit for CSE exams, while the white children are encouraged to take O levels. Your son is Nigerian and wants to take certain O levels. He is perfectly capable of doing so, but is not allowed to attend the O level classes.

A black child and a white child are caught bullying other children at school. Both have been equally disruptive and troublesome in the past. The black child is suspended from school, the white child is not. This is a fairly common problem and one to look out for. A recent investigation in Birmingham showed that black pupils were four times more likely to be suspended than white ones. They were suspended on average at a younger age, and after shorter periods and fewer incidents of disruption. They were also less likely to be readmitted to schools. (The circumstances in which discrimination may be lawful are described below.)

What can I do if my child is racially abused or assaulted by other pupils?

You cannot take any legal action against the school, but there are other steps you can take to ensure that it is stopped.

The first thing to do is to bring it to the notice of the headmaster or headmistress and demand that disciplinary action be taken against the pupils involved. If your child is physically assaulted, report the matter to the police as well. Although the police are unlikely to take any action, it is important that the matter be officially recorded.

If no action is taken against the perpetrators, and the attacks and the abuse continue, the only thing to do is to involve other organizations and start a campaign so that pressure can be brought to bear upon the local education authority, the school and the police to do something. There are black groups and organizations throughout the country who would be willing to organize or become involved in a campaign. You may also get some support or assistance from your local Community Relations Council.

The important thing is not to sit back and take it. Do something.

What can I do if the school uses racist books or teaches subjects in a racist way?

Again, you cannot take any legal action against the school. It really means changing attitudes, traditions and teaching patterns which have developed over many years and are now fairly deeply entrenched. Change can only be brought about by teachers, parents and students getting together and pushing for a multi-cultural and anti-racist curriculum.

The only way in which you as parents can get anything done is by keeping in close contact with the school, knowing what is going on, liaising with other parents and the teachers, making formal complaints and letting your objections be known to the local education authority and the governors of the school. The same applies if you wish to take action in respect of a teacher or a headmaster or headmistress who has expressed racist views.

If you are a teacher and are opposed to the use of racist books and racist teaching methods, bring these to the notice of your union, and try to get their support to change the existing practice.

What can be done if the school discriminates against a teacher?

If you are a teacher and a school discriminates racially against you in relation to recruitment, promotion or dismissal, you are suffering from discrimination as an employee. You can, therefore, bring proceedings for it in an industrial tribunal against your employer. Your employer will be either the local education authority, or the governors or managers of the school, depending on who was responsible for the relevant act of discrimination (see Chapters 2 and 4).

Parents and students can, of course, support the teacher by organizing a campaign and bringing pressure to bear upon the school and the local education authority.

Who is responsible for race discrimination in schools?

If the school in question is maintained by a local education authority, the body responsible for race discrimination will be the local education authority or the managers or governors of the school, depending on whose duty it was to carry out the act about which you are complaining.

If the school is an independent school or a special school which is not maintained by a local education authority, the person responsible will be the proprietor, that is, the person or body of persons responsible for the management of the school.

In either case, the relevant body will also be responsible for any acts of discrimination by any of its employees, i.e. the headmaster or headmistress or teachers, unless it can show that it took such steps as were reasonably practicable to stop the person in question behaving in a discriminatory way.

What is unlawful discrimination in further education?

'Further education' covers a large number of institutions that provide education, training or instruction after you leave school. It includes universities, polytechnics, colleges and other educational establishments either maintained by local education authorities or funded by the Department of Education and Science. Whether the establishment provides full-time or part-time education is irrelevant; any reference to a university includes its hall(s) of residence.

It is unlawful for any of the above institutions to discriminate racially against you either by not offering you a place or by offering to do so on less favourable terms than to other students. A simple example of this would be where a black student and a white one apply to a polytechnic to read law. Both have the same number of A levels, although the black student has far better grades than the white one. The white student is given a place while the black is not.

If you are already a student at one of these institutions, it is unlawful for them to discriminate racially against you by not allowing you to take certain courses or attend certain classes, by refusing you access to any of the other benefits, facilities and services which they provide, or by treating you unfavourably in any other way. This means that discrimination is illegal not only on the academic front, but also in other aspects of your life at the institution.

On the academic front, it covers the options of courses which you are offered, the quality of the teaching which you receive and the assessment of your work. If your options as a black student are restricted, compared to those of the white students, the quality of your teaching poor and your assessments low in spite of your ability and the calibre of your work, you are being unlawfully discriminated against.

On the non-academic side it covers things such as the provision of accommodation, access to and the use of libraries and sports facilities, and the hiring of rooms for meetings and parties. If there is segregation in the provision of accommodation, or the black or overseas students are provided with poorer accommodation, it is unlawful. The same applies if the Pakistan Society at a university is refused permission to hire a particular room for a meeting when the same room has in the past been hired by white student organizations for their meetings.

Are there any circumstances in which discrimination in education is permitted?

There are four main areas in which discrimination is lawful.

(a) An independent school or college which was set up or is funded by a charitable trust may discriminate in its admissions policy in order to give effect to the terms of the trust, except that it may not do so on the basis of colour. Similarly, any educational establishment may discriminate in the giving of awards and scholarships to fulfil the terms of the charitable trust which created them. Again it must not discriminate on the basis of colour. The following examples show what this means.

An independent school in Wales is entirely funded by a charitable trust which was set up to provide education for Welsh-speaking children. Thus, one of the requirements for entering that school is that you must be Welsh-speaking. You are a West Indian and, not surprisingly, your children do not speak any Welsh. Your daughter is refused entrance to that school. Although this is indirect discrimination against West Indians, it is perfectly lawful. Had the trust been set up to provide education for white Welsh-speaking children, the school would have had to ignore the reference to 'white'. The refusal to admit a black Welsh-speaking child would be unlawful race discrimination.

You are a Pakistani and your child attends a school in Bradford. Every year the school gives an award to students who get into Oxford. Your son gets into Oxford, but does not get the award. The terms of the charitable trust which provides the award are that it must be given to a student who was born in Yorkshire. Your son was born in Pakistan. The school has acted lawfully in not giving your son the award. If the terms of the trust had been that the award should be given to a 'white student born in Yorkshire' the school could only legally give effect to it by ignoring the reference to colour. If it had refused to give the award to a Pakistani student born in Yorkshire, it would have broken the law and its conduct would have been unlawful race discrimination.

(b) A school or any other educational establishment acts lawfully if it discriminates positively by providing facilities or services to meet the special needs of a particular racial group with regard to their education or training. For example, if a school sets up special English classes for children whose first language is not English, it is acting lawfully. An English child who is not allowed to attend those classes cannot complain of race discrimination.

(c) An educational establishment can discriminate positively in its admissions policy in favour of students who are not ordinarily resident in Britain and who, it appears to the establishment, do not intend to remain in Britain after having completed their studies. Thus a university acts lawfully if it reserves a certain number of places for overseas students or if it imposes lower entry requirements for overseas students than it does for English students. An English student who does not get a place at the university for either of these reasons cannot complain of race discrimination. This remains the position even if the overseas student subsequently remains in Britain. If you are an overseas student, what matters is what the university thought your intention was at the time when it admitted you. If it believed *at the time* that you would return to your country after completing your degree, it acted lawfully.

(d) Discrimination by educational establishments is lawful if it is permitted by an Act of Parliament or Regulations made by a Minister (see page 106). Thus it is lawful to charge overseas students (those who have not been ordinarily resident in the UK or the EEC for three years immediately prior to starting their course) higher fees and to say that they are not entitled to a grant because the Minister of Education has made regulations to that effect.

What is unlawful discrimination by local education authorities?

It is unlawful for local education authorities to discriminate racially in carrying out any of their functions. They carry out a large number of functions, some of which are compulsory, others discretionary.

Each local education authority has to make sure that its area has sufficient nursery, primary, secondary and special schools, that the premises of every school maintained by them conform to the prescribed standards and include adequate facilities for recreation and physical training. It is impossible here to outline all the duties of local education authorities, but some of them relate to non-attendance at school, medical inspections and the provision of meals and transport.

Local education authorities are also responsible for giving grants to students for further education. In some cases you are automatically entitled to a grant, provided of course that you satisfy the residence requirements (see page 67). In other cases, the local education authority has a discretion as to whether or not to give you a grant. It must not use any discriminatory criteria in deciding when to give a grant. The following are examples of unlawful discrimination by local education authorities.

Black families in a certain district all live in the same catchment area and, therefore, all their children attend the same school. The school has sixty per cent black students and forty per cent white. The local education authority believes that it is undesirable to have too many black students in any one school, and feels that it is much better if they are distributed evenly among the schools in the district. Therefore, in order to 'promote integration', they decide to send some of the black students to schools outside the catchment area. Nothing relating to the education of the children requires such a move. Such a 'dispersal policy' would be unlawful discrimination.

In deciding whether a child is 'educationally subnormal' and needs to attend a special school, one of the criteria used by the local education authority is the child's ability to read and write in English. A child who has recently come over from Pakistan and is of average intelligence is classified as educationally subnormal simply because of her poor command of the English language. This is unlawful discrimination because the criterion used is discriminatory and has no bearing on the question of intelligence and the ability to learn.

What can I do if I or my child have been discriminated against?
You can bring proceedings for race discrimination in the County Court (see Chapter 8 for details of how to bring proceedings).

If your complaint is about race discrimination in the public sector of education – a state school, a special school, a polytechnic or a college maintained by the local education authority or funded by the Department of Education and Science – you must first of all give notice of it in writing to the Secretary of State for Education. The reasoning behind this is that, since the Secretary of State has ultimate responsibility for education in the public sector, he/she must first be given an opportunity to conduct inquiries and, if he/she finds that there is discrimination, to take steps to eradicate it. In practice, it is extremely unlikely that he/she will ever find that there has been any discrimination. You cannot start proceedings unless either the Secretary of State has written to you and informed you that he/she does not require further time to consider the matter, or two months have passed since you wrote to him/her. In such a case you must start proceedings within eight months of the act of discrimination taking place.

If the complaint is about a university or an independent school or college, you do not need to give notice to the Secretary of State, but must start proceedings within six months of the act of discrimination taking place. In certain circumstances when assistance is being sought from the Commission for Racial Equality, this period may be extended to eight or nine months (see page 97).

Before deciding to start proceedings, write to the responsible body pointing out the discrimination and the fact that it is unlawful, and state that unless it is dealt with, you intend to start proceedings. This may have the desired effect, and it would be quicker and easier than bringing proceedings in court.

If you feel that the discrimination is not an isolated incident, but, for example, is symptomatic of the way a particular institution treats black students, inform the

Commission for Racial Equality about it (for their address, see page 40). Write to them giving details of as many incidents as possible. You may have some reservations about the CRE, but remember that they are the only body with the resources and the powers to conduct formal investigations, obtain information and make recommendations.

6: Housing and Premises

Is race discrimination in housing unlawful?

Yes. Subject to the exceptions below, it is unlawful for anyone who owns property, or anyone authorized by the owner to sell or let it, to discriminate racially against you if you are trying to acquire housing accommodation. It is also unlawful for the owner or anyone who manages the property for him, to discriminate racially against you if you are already in occupation.

What about land and business premises?

Race discrimination in the disposal of land and business premises is unlawful in the same way. However, as most problems arise in relation to housing, this chapter will concentrate on that aspect, although almost everything said here will apply equally to the disposal of land and business premises.

Does it make any difference whether I am buying or renting the property?

No, the way in which you acquire the property is entirely irrelevant, as indeed is the size, quality and type of property. Race discrimination is unlawful whether you are buying a freehold or a leasehold, or renting the property. Your tenancy could be a long one or a short one, it could be for a fixed period or for an indefinite period requiring weekly or monthly payments of rent.

It is equally immaterial whether the property in question is a house, a flat or a bed-sit. If, however, it is a bed-sit or a flat which is not self-contained (that is, you have to share certain amenities) and the landlord or his family live there as well, it may be classified as 'small premises' (see page 78). If that is the case, race discrimination in respect of it will not be against the law.

It is also irrelevant if the property in question is not immediately available for occupation. Thus, it is unlawful for property companies developing housing estates to discriminate in the selling of houses, even if they do so before the houses are complete and ready for occupation.

Who are the people who must not discriminate?

First, there must not be any race discrimination by the person who owns the relevant property. The owner could be a private individual, a commercial organization, a local authority or a housing association.

The owner is also responsible for acts of discrimination by employees, unless he or she can show that such steps were taken as were reasonably practicable to stop the employee discriminating.

For example, you are the only Indian family living in a block of flats. The landlord company employs a porter, one of whose tasks is to collect the rubbish from outside each flat every day. The porter collects everybody else's rubbish, but refuses to collect yours. You complain to the landlord company several times, but the position remains unchanged. In such a situation, the landlord company is responsible for the porter's discrimination.

In certain cases, the day-to-day management of the property may have been delegated by the owner to someone else. A large commercial landlord may delegate the management of a large block of flats to another company. In such a case, the landlord company is responsible for the actions of their property managers which are done with their authority.

Second, there must not be any race discrimination by agencies which are entrusted with the selling or renting of property. A person who wants to sell his house or flat often uses an estate agent to find him a buyer; similarly, a person wishing to let property often uses accommodation agencies or bureaux to find tenants. The following is an example of unlawful discrimination by an estate agent.

You are a Nigerian and you see a 'for sale' sign outside a house with a particular estate agent's name on it. You go to see the estate agent to inquire about that property, but are told that it has already been sold. Suspecting that the estate agent has not been entirely honest with you, you get a friend to call a short while later and ask if that house is still available. Your friend is told that it is and is given an appointment to see it the following day.

Agencies usually discriminate in this way because they have been instructed to do so by the landlord. If you decide to bring proceedings in such a case, ascertain who the landlord is and issue proceedings against the landlord as well as the estate agent. The landlord is equally responsible for anything the estate agent does with his/her authority.

If you work for an estate agent or accommodation bureau and are given racist instructions by a landlord, you can report the landlord to the Commission for Racial Equality (CRE). It is unlawful for the landlord to instruct you to discriminate on racial grounds. This is something in respect of which individuals cannot take any action, but the CRE can (see Chapter 10).

Third, it is unlawful for other tenants to instruct or bring pressure to bear upon the landlord to discriminate racially against you. For instance, you are a black family and about to be allocated a flat on a particular council estate. The white tenants on that estate sign a petition, asking the local authority not to allocate that flat to you. Their actions are unlawful. Again, this is a matter in respect of which you as an individual cannot take any legal action, but the CRE can. So report it to the CRE, providing as much detail as you can. If the local authority gives in to the tenants and does not allocate that particular flat to you, then that local authority, as the owner of the property, is unlawfully discriminating against you. This is so even if it claims that it had your best interests at heart and did not want you to live on an estate where you might have been the victim of racial harassment.

Finally, anyone who publishes a discriminatory advertisement is also breaking the law (see page 110). Only the CRE can bring proceedings for this, so if you see such an advertisement report it to them.

What is unlawful discrimination when I am looking for accommodation?

There are three ways in which race discrimination against you in connection with finding somewhere to live will be unlawful. First, a landlord (or landlady) or any of a landlord's agents must not on racial grounds refuse to sell or rent the property to you. The following examples show how such discrimination normally takes place.

You are of Afro-Caribbean origin and are looking for a flat to rent. Seeing one advertised in your local newspaper, you telephone the landlord and are told that the flat is still vacant. You arrange to see it half an hour later. When you arrive, the landlord takes one look at you and says that someone else came to see it after you called and that the flat has been let to that person. This kind of discrimination, which occurs quite often, is normally fairly easy to prove. Not only does the landlord's explanation seem incredible, bearing in mind the short gap between your call and your visit to the premises, but also the landlord will probably not be in a position to supply the name and address of the person who is allegedly the new tenant of the flat, let alone call the person in question as a witness. If you suspect the landlord of lying, it may be a good idea to get a friend to call a short time later to enquire about the flat.

You are white and respond to a newspaper advertisement for a flat to let. You go to see the landlord, who is quite happy to rent you the flat. In the course of conversation you mention that you will be sharing the flat with a friend. When he learns that your friend is Pakistani, the landlord refuses to let you have the flat because he says he has had trouble in the past with Pakistani tenants. This is unlawful race discrimination against you on the basis of your friend's colour.

Second, landlords or their agents must not discriminate racially against you by offering to sell or rent you the property on less favourable terms than they do to others. For instance, you are an Indian couple and want to rent a flat. The landlord agrees to rent the flat to you, but asks you to pay a certain deposit. You discover that the white tenants in the same building either did not have to pay a deposit at all or paid less than you. Other examples of 'less favourable terms' would be charging black tenants higher rents, although the accommodation provided for them is identical to that provided for the white tenants; asking for someone to guarantee the rent when white tenants do not have to provide a guarantor; or imposing greater repairing obligations upon them.

Third, an estate agent or accommodation bureau must not discriminate racially against you in relation to any lists they have of people looking for premises to buy or rent. For example, an accommodation bureau has a list of people looking for single bed-sits in West

Hampstead; there are white as well as black people on the list. It would be unlawful for them to treat the black people on the list in any way less favourably than the white people. This would apply, for instance, if the white people are sent lists of bed-sits which are in a better state of repair than the ones sent to the black people, or if the black people are only sent to bed-sits owned by black landlords.

What is unlawful discrimination when I am in occupation?

It is unlawful for a landlord, or anyone managing the premises for that landlord, to treat you less favourably than the other tenants on racial grounds. This also applies to being evicted from the premises. The following are examples of unlawful discrimination.

White and Asian families live in a block of flats which has a communal garden. Whenever the Asian children play in the garden, they are racially abused and beaten by some of the white teenagers. On occasions the police are called in, but they take no action. The landlord's answer to the problem is to tell the Asian families not to use the garden any more.

A West Indian and a white tenant fall into arrears with their rent. This is the first time that it has happened to either of them, and the arrears are approximately the same in both cases. The landlord starts possession proceedings against the West Indian tenant, but not against the white.

What if the landlord does not allow me to sub-let to a black person?

Most tenancies include a term about sub-letting. In some cases it is prohibited altogether – you are not allowed to sub-let to anyone. In other cases, you are allowed to sub-let provided that you get the consent of the landlord to do so. The landlord must not refuse consent unless there is reasonable justification for doing so (see *The Private Tenant's Handbook* or *The Public Tenant's Handbook* in this series).

If a landlord refuses consent because the proposed sub-tenant is black, this is unlawful discrimination against that person. In such a case, there are two things which can be done. First, the prospective black sub-tenant can bring proceedings for race discrimination against the landlord in the County Court. Second, you can apply to the County Court for an order declaring that the landlord's refusal to consent is unreasonable, and that you are allowed to sub-let.

The same applies if you are assigning (transferring) your tenancy to someone else. People with long leases often regard themselves as the 'owners' of the property in question, and talk of 'buying' and 'selling' it. What you in fact do when you 'sell' the property is assign your long lease to someone else. Thus if the freeholder (the landlord) refuses to consent to your selling (assigning) the premises to a black person, the landlord is unlawfully discriminating against that person.

If the premises in question are 'small premises' and amenities have to be shared with the landlord or a member of the landlord's family (see page 78), the prospective sub-tenants or assignees can not complain of race discrimination. It is still, however, open to you as the tenant to seek a declaration that the consent is being unreasonably withheld.

Are there any circumstances in which race discrimination is permitted?

Yes. Race discrimination is not unlawful if it takes place in any of the following circumstances.

First, a landlord can refuse to have black tenants, or

to sub-let to black people, if *all* the following three conditions are fulfilled:

(a) Either the landlord or a 'near relative' of the landlord's lives on the premises and intends to continue doing so. The term 'near relative' refers to the landlord's wife or husband, parent, child, grandparent, grandchild, brother or sister. It applies equally to half-brothers and half-sisters, illegitimate children and the spouses of illegitimate children.

(b) The landlord or a near relative has to share certain accommodation with the other people living there. The shared accommodation must be something other than a common entrance-hall or staircase or storage accommodation. Thus it could be a kitchen, a bathroom or a lavatory.

(c) The premises are 'small premises'. This could mean either that the premises are divided in such a way as to provide accommodation for no more than three households, one of which is occupied by the landlord or near relative, or that there is accommodation on the premises for no more than six persons in addition to the landlord or near relative. The following examples show what this means.

The landlord and family live in a flat on the ground floor. There are two flats on the first floor, one of which is let to a young couple with a child, the other is vacant. All three flats share a bathroom. The landlord does not break the law if he refuses to let the third flat to a black family. If, however, there had been another flat on the second floor, the landlord's discrimination would have been unlawful.

The landlord's mother occupies two rooms in a large house. There are six other rooms which are let to students. The landlord's mother shares a kitchen and a dining-room with the lodgers. The landlord's refusal to have any black lodgers is lawful. If, however, there had been a seventh room in the house which could also be let, then his race discrimination would have been unlawful.

Secondly, an owner-occupier – that is, someone who lives in the relevant house or flat and is either a freeholder or has a long lease in respect of it – can discriminate racially in disposing of it, as long as an estate agent is not used to do so, and the sale is not advertised in any other way. If a 'for sale' sign is put up outside that property, then that sign is advertising its sale and, therefore, discrimination would be unlawful. This exception envisages a purely private transaction, and it is very unlikely that you would even know that it was taking place.

Third, charitable housing trusts and associations can discriminate on racial grounds, so long as this is not on the basis of colour, to give effect to the terms of a trust (see page 108).

Finally, a landlord or a landlord's agent does not break the law if the race discrimination relates to property outside Britain. Thus, a person in this country who owns a villa in Portugal is entitled to discriminate in terms of race when selling or renting it, even though the sale or letting takes place in this country.

What can I do about race discrimination by local authorities?

A local authority, when carrying out its functions in relation to the provision of housing, is in exactly the same position as a private landlord, and race discrimination by it is unlawful in exactly the same way. Housing in London is usually provided by the London Borough Councils; outside London, it is usually provided by district councils. It is unlawful for them to discriminate racially in the provision of council housing or against council tenants.

Race discrimination by local authorities does not often involve a single clear definable act. If it does, there is nothing to prevent you taking proceedings against it in a County Court, just as you would do against a private landlord. You could do this, for instance, if a local authority had a requirement that in order to be placed on its waiting-list, you must have been resident in the UK for a year. As a Pakistani who arrived in the UK some six months ago, you could argue that this was indirect discrimination. Or you could allege direct discrimination if the local authority started possession proceedings against you, a black tenant, but did not do so against a white tenant who was in exactly the same position as you.

However, before you start any proceedings, try taking the matter up with a senior officer or councillor of the local authority, either personally or through a law centre or some other advice agency. This may bring about the desired result, and it would be considerably cheaper and quicker than going through the courts.

Most allegations of race discrimination against local authorities are, however, likely to be much more complicated, and will probably involve looking at the authority's policies and practices over a lengthy period. This may well mean making a careful study of persons requiring accommodation, their personal circumstances and history as council tenants, the accommodation available and the local authority's resources. The following examples show the kind of situations in which such difficulties could arise.

You have reason to believe from your personal experience that a local authority treats black people less favourably in the allocation of council housing, in that they have to wait longer for accommodation and are eventually allocated poorer housing.

You are an Asian council tenant. All the other families

in the same block of flats as you are also Asian. The block of flats opposite yours appears to house only white families. You believe that the local authority is operating a segregation policy.

Your application to be transferred to a particular council estate is refused on the ground that there are already too many blacks on that estate. You believe that the local authority is operating a 'dispersal policy', whereby it only allocates housing to a specific number of blacks on each estate.

The last two examples may even be well intentioned. The purpose of the former may be to enable people of the same culture who speak the same language to provide mutual support to each other. The purpose of the latter may be to promote integration and avoid racial tension. The motives of the local authority are, however, irrelevant. What is important is that people should not be treated differently because of their race or colour.

If a local authority is doing any of the above it is discriminating unlawfully. However, it would be virtually impossible for you as an individual to take on the task of proving it. What you can do, though, is to report it to the Commission for Racial Equality, providing as much detail as possible. They have the resources and the powers to conduct formal investigations, publish reports, make recommendations and issue non-discrimination notices (see Chapter 11).

What can I do about racial harassment by other council tenants?

There are three main areas of action open to you.

First, report the matter to the police, especially if there has been physical assault of any kind. The police may not charge the persons responsible, but at least your complaint will have been noted and recorded.

This may be helpful if you decide to take other proceedings at a later date. If you suffer any injuries as a result of an attack, even if it is a small bruise or a graze, see your doctor while the injury is still visible and, if possible, try and have it photographed.

Second, take the matter up with the relevant local authority. Local authorities can start possession proceedings against a tenant if they or anyone living with them have been guilty of conduct which is a nuisance or annoyance to their neighbours. A person who racially harasses their neighbours is undoubtedly guilty of such conduct. You cannot compel the local authority to bring proceedings against the relevant tenant, but you can bring pressure upon it to do so.

Increasing numbers of local authorities now have a racial harassment clause as part of their tenancy agreements. The effect of this is that someone who racially harasses their neighbours is in breach of their tenancy agreement, and the local authority can start possession proceedings on this basis. If your local authority does not have such a clause in its tenancy agreements, try to bring pressure on it to do so.

Finally, if neither the police nor the local authority take any action against the tenants who have been harassing you, you can start legal proceedings yourself. You can start either criminal proceedings or civil proceedings.

Criminal proceedings are always started in the magistrates' court, although in certain cases the defendant can choose to have his case tried in a Crown Court. It will be up to you to bring the prosecution and to prove the case against the other tenant. You will not get any legal aid to do so; thus if you want to be legally represented – and it is advisable that you are – you will have to pay for it. In addition, if the other tenant is acquitted, you will also be ordered to pay their costs. If they are convicted, they will probably have to pay a small fine. There would generally be nothing to stop them harassing you again.

Take legal advice before starting criminal proceedings. Only if you have a very strong case which is supported by good witnesses, medical evidence and photographs, should you start criminal proceedings.

The far better solution is to start civil proceedings in a County Court for assault, and ask the court to grant an injunction and damages. An injunction is an order of the court which will specify certain things which the other tenant should not do, such as assault, molest or otherwise interfere with you. 'Damages' is the amount of money which the court feels should be awarded to you for the wrong that has been done to you.

It will probably take several months before your case is heard in court. If you want to do something to stop the harassment in the meantime, you can apply to the court for what is known as an 'interim' injunction. You can only do this once you have started proceedings in the County Court.

If the other tenant continues to harass you after you have got an injunction (and that includes an 'interim' injunction), this is a contempt of court, and you can take the tenant back to the County Court to be dealt with for it. Theoretically, that tenant can be sent to prison, although in practice this very rarely happens.

The main advantage of bringing proceedings in the County Court is that you can get legal aid to do so, depending of course on your means. Legal aid will cover all your legal costs. If you are legally aided and lose your case, you will not normally be ordered to pay the other side's costs.

Where do I bring proceedings for discrimination in housing?

Proceedings should be brought in a County Court, and you must normally start them within six months of the act of discrimination (see Chapter 8 for details of how to bring proceedings in a County Court).

7: Goods, Facilities, Services and Associations

What are 'goods, facilities and services'?
In the preceding chapters we have dealt with discrimination in connection with your work (Chapters 2 and 3), your or your children's education (Chapter 5) and your home (Chapter 6). The other main area in which you are likely to suffer discrimination in everyday life will be in relation to the provision of 'goods, facilities and services'. This vague and general phrase covers almost everything you do in your daily life – things that you do for pleasure as well as things that have to be done out of necessity.

There is no special legal meaning attached to the words 'goods', 'facilities' or 'services'. They have the same meaning in this context as they do ordinarily. The meaning of 'goods' is obvious and needs no further elaboration. Providing 'facilities' simply means making available to you the opportunity to do something or to get some benefit. 'Services' are provided when work is done to meet some general needs.

What is unlawful discrimination in the provision of goods?
It is unlawful for anyone who is concerned with the provision of goods to the public, or to a section of it, to discriminate against you because of your race either by not providing you with the goods or by treating you in some other way less favourably than the other customers.

Any shop (whether it is a showroom selling cars or a

local greengrocer selling vegetables) is concerned with providing goods to the public. So indeed are market stalls and those who sell goods through mail catalogues. An example of someone providing goods to a section of the public is a wholesaler who sells only to retailers and not to the public at large.

It is very unlikely that any salesperson will discriminate against you by refusing to sell you their goods – after all, racists don't usually distinguish when it comes to the colour of money. They are more likely to discriminate against you by treating you less favourably in other ways. The following examples indicate the type of situations in which you may be the victim of unlawful discrimination.

A West Indian buys a cassette recorder from a particular shop. He is not satisfied with it and takes it back the following day. He wants to exchange it for another cassette recorder or, failing that, to be given a refund for it. The sales assistant tells him that it is the company's policy not to exchange goods or give refunds. A short while later he sees another sales assistant exchanging goods for a white customer.

An Indian woman, settled and living in the UK, buys furniture from a department store. She inquires about credit terms and she is asked if she can provide a reference or the name of someone to guarantee the payments. A white person who buys on credit from the same store is not asked to provide a reference or a guarantor.

A Pakistani buys a washing machine from a shop. He asks whether it can be delivered to his house and is told that it cannot because he does not live within five miles of the shop. His neighbour, who is white, buys a fridge from the same shop and it is delivered by them to his house.

What is unlawful discrimination in the provision of facilities?

It is unlawful for anyone who is concerned with providing facilities to the general public, or to a section of it, to discriminate racially against you either by refusing to provide you with the facilities or by not providing you with facilities of the same quality, in the same manner and on the same terms as are normally provided to other people.

The phrase 'provision of facilities' covers a wide range of activities in various spheres of your life, and it is impossible to give a complete list of all of them. The following questions may give an indication of the kind of things which are covered by this phrase.

Is it unlawful for places providing refreshments and/or entertainment to discriminate?

Yes, because they are open to the general public and provide them with facilities to eat, drink and enjoy themselves. Thus it is unlawful for restaurants, cafés, wine bars, pubs, cinemas, theatres, concert halls, discothèques and night clubs to discriminate against you by refusing you entrance or by not serving you.

The two areas where discrimination occurs most frequently are in pubs and night clubs/discothèques. The following are examples of unlawful discrimination.

A publican refuses to serve a turbaned Sikh customer, and asks him to leave the pub. The explanation given is that a 'no hats' rule operates in the pub. This is indirect discrimination.

The landlord of a small pub where all the locals know each other refuses to serve a group of Bengalis. His explanation is that they do not mingle with the other customers, but sit together in a corner, talking in their own language. He claims that this offends his other customers. This is direct discrimination.

The doorman of a club refuses entrance to two black youths on the ground that they are not wearing ties. Five minutes later, two white youths, who are also not wearing ties, are allowed into the club. This is direct discrimination. Night clubs and discothèques often try to show that they were not discriminating on racial grounds by producing evidence that there were black people in the club on the night in question. The thing to watch out for is that many clubs operate a 'quota system' whereby a certain number of black people are allowed in every night. The use of such a quota system is unlawful race discrimination.

The other common ploy used by clubs to refuse black people entrance is to tell them that they are a members only club, and do not admit non-members. The only way to expose this is to send some white friends to the club on the following night and see if they are told the same thing.

It is also unlawful for a club or a pub to ban *all* black people from entering simply because two black customers got into a fight one night.

Which other places are concerned with providing facilities?

There are many different places where people go to indulge in various pastimes and leisure activities. These include bingo halls, bookmakers, amusement arcades, fitness and exercise centres, swimming pools, parks, museums and libraries. These are all concerned with providing facilities. If they are open to the public, or to a section of it, then race discrimination by them is illegal.

If a university library is open only to its own students, it is providing facilities to a section of the public, namely to students at that particular university. If it treats a black student any less favourably than a white student, this is unlawful race discrimination. The same applies to women-only swimming pools – black women must not be treated less favourably than white women.

Is race discrimination by banks and building societies unlawful?

Yes, it is unlawful for banks, building societies, financial companies or anyone else who is involved in giving loans, grants or credit, to discriminate racially in the provision of any of their facilities.

This means that banks and building societies must not discriminate in such matters as arranging overdraft facilities and giving loans (this includes mortgages). The following is an example of direct discrimination by a bank. An African and a white of similar financial standing and in similar employment both apply to the same bank for overdraft facilities of £1,000. The white person is granted that facility; the African is only allowed an overdraft of up to £300. Unless there is some good explanation for the different treatment, the bank has discriminated unlawfully.

Discrimination in the giving of mortgages is more likely to be indirect than direct. For instance, a building society in a certain town has a policy not to lend money on properties in a particular area. The area in question has a substantial Asian population, and therefore provides amenities which cater for their needs. Most of the Asians in that town who wish to buy property want to do so in that area. Hardly any of the whites in that town want to buy property there. The building society's lending practice thus has an adverse effect on the town's Asian community, and this is indirect race discrimination.

It is also unlawful for local authorities to discriminate racially in the giving of loans and grants, and for shops and businesses to discriminate in the giving of credit.

Race discrimination, however, is perfectly legal if it relates to someone trying to raise finance for a purpose which is going to be carried out outside Britain. For example, an Indian and an American of similar financial standing both try to raise finance with a London bank in order to buy property in New York; the American succeeds, but the Indian fails. Although the bank has discriminated racially against the Indian, it has not broken the law.

Is race discrimination by insurance companies unlawful?

Yes, it is unlawful for insurance companies to discriminate against you on racial grounds either by refusing to give you a policy or by charging you a higher premium than they charge their other clients. Thus insurance companies act unlawfully if they refuse to give motor insurance policies to people who were not born in the UK, or if they charge higher premiums to foreign nationals or charge on the basis of the length of their residence in this country. For example, an Indian national aged thirty has lived in Britain since she was eight years old. She learned to drive in this country and holds a British driving licence. The insurance company would be breaking the law if they charged her a higher premium simply on the basis of her nationality.

Insurance companies, however, do not break the law if they discriminate on racial grounds by refusing to give a policy, if the policy in question is in respect of risks which are going to arise wholly or mainly outside Britain.

Do hotels break the law if they refuse to give rooms to black people?

Yes, because it is unlawful for anyone providing accommodation to the public, or to a section of it, to discriminate on racial grounds.

Discrimination in the provision of accommodation is fairly common in smaller hotels and boarding houses. Their normal tactic, upon seeing a black person, is simply to say that they are fully booked and have no rooms available. If this happens to you and you suspect race discrimination, get a white friend either to telephone or to go to the hotel to ask for a room. If this person is given a room, you are in a stronger position to prove the race discrimination. Otherwise, all you have is a suspicion with nothing to substantiate it.

Discrimination, however, is not unlawful if the boarding house or hotel cannot accommodate more than six people, and if the owner or a near relative lives there and shares certain amenities, such as a kitchen, bathroom or lavatory, with the other residents (for the meaning of 'a near relative', see page 78).

What is unlawful discrimination in the provision of services?

It is unlawful for anyone concerned with the provision of services to the public, or to a section of it, to discriminate racially against you either by not providing you with the services or by providing you with services of inferior quality or on less favourable terms than they normally do.

The following are examples of people concerned with the provision of services: people who provide 'professional' services, such as doctors, accountants, dentists, solicitors and surveyors; people who provide you with the skilled services of a trade, such as builders, carpenters, plumbers, electricians and car mechanics; and people who tend your welfare needs, such as social workers, probation officers and health visitors.

If you are discriminated against by a professional person, you can, of course, always complain to the relevant professional body which regulates the conduct of its members – the Law Society for solicitors, the General Medical Council for doctors, etc. Most professional bodies, unfortunately, have not made race discrimination a disciplinary offence in itself, but it should, if proved, amount to professional misconduct. There is, of course, nothing to stop you bringing proceedings in the County Court as you would against anyone else who had discriminated against you in the provision of services.

What if the discrimination relates to the provision of goods, facilities or services abroad?

Generally, you cannot bring any proceedings for race discrimination in this country for goods, facilities or services which are provided abroad. There are, however, two exceptions to that.

First, you can complain if someone in Britain discriminates racially against you in the provision of travel facilities abroad. For instance, a tour operator in London offers package holidays to Kenya, which includes flights and accommodation. Upon arrival in Kenya, the black members of the group find that, although they paid the same as their white counterparts, they have been booked into cheaper and inferior hotels. This is unlawful conduct by the tour operator because the act of discrimination took place in London when the hotel bookings were made.

Second, you can complain if the discrimination takes place on board a British ship, aircraft or hovercraft. Thus you could complain if there was segregation on a British Airways flight or if black passengers on a British ship were not given access to the same facilities as the white passengers.

Are there any circumstances in which discrimination is lawful?

There are three main areas in which race discrimination in the provision of goods, facilities and services is not against the law.

First, those who are party to arrangements under which (for payment or not) they take into their home and treat as members of their family, children, old people or people requiring a special degree of care and attention, do not act unlawfully if they discriminate on racial grounds. This applies, for instance, to white foster parents refusing to foster black children; that is perfectly legal, even though it is something in respect of which they are paid.

Second, it is lawful to discriminate positively to provide facilities or services only to persons of a particular racial group, if this is done to meet some special need in regard to their welfare. For example, anyone involved in the setting up of a women's refuge (home for battered women) solely for Asian women would be acting lawfully. The obvious reason for that is that Asian women who are the victims of domestic violence have difficulties which other women in the same position don't share. In addition to practical problems, such as language difficulties, there are the special traumas and pressures which come from having been brought up in a particular culture which has a different set of values from those found in a western culture.

Finally, any race discrimination which occurs as a result of following the terms of a charitable instrument is lawful, so long as it is not on the basis of colour (see page 108). Thus a home set up under a charitable trust for single Jamaican mothers is lawful. On the other hand, a home set up for single black mothers is not.

Is race discrimination by a members' club unlawful?

It is unlawful for any association (and that includes clubs) which has twenty-five or more members, to discriminate on the grounds of race against either its members or associates or those applying to join it. This covers social clubs where one can eat, drink or dance; clubs where one can play sports or games; political organizations; and any other group which has a constitution defining who is eligible for membership and how such a person can join. You are an 'associate' of a club or organization if you are entitled under its constitution to enjoy some or all of the rights of members even though, in fact, you are not a member.

A club breaks the law if, on racial grounds, it refuses your application for membership or is prepared to admit you on less favourable terms than other members. The latter would apply, for instance, where a club stipulated that you could join so long as you only used its facilities at certain times.

If you are already a member or associate of a club, it is unlawful for the club to discriminate racially against you in any way. For example, an Indian member and a white member of a social club get very drunk one night and cause some damage to the club. Neither has caused any trouble before. The Indian is deprived of membership, the white isn't. Unless there is a good reason for the different treatment, this is unlawful race discrimination.

Is it unlawful for ethnic groups to set up their own organizations?

No, you can do so as long as your main object is to confer benefits on persons of a particular racial group. You can then restrict your membership to persons of that racial group. The group, however, must not be defined by reference to colour. It is, therefore, perfectly legal to have social, welfare, political or sporting organizations which exist primarily to confer benefits on a particular ethnic or national group, and which limit their membership to persons of that group. Thus a West Indian or an English person who is not allowed to join the Indian Workers' Association or an Asian arts group cannot complain of race discrimination.

What can I do if I have been discriminated against?

You can bring proceedings in the County Court, but must normally do so within six months of the act of discrimination taking place (see Chapter 8 for details of how to bring proceedings in the County Court).

8: Proceedings in the County Court

When do I bring proceedings in the County Court?

If you have suffered race discrimination in education (see Chapter 5), housing (see Chapter 6) or the provision of goods, facilities and services (see Chapter 7), you can start legal proceedings against the discriminator in a County Court.

In which County Court do I start proceedings?

There are two things to remember when selecting the right County Court in which to bring your case. First, not all County Courts can hear race discrimination cases. Your case can only be tried in a County Court which has been specifically designated to hear race discrimination cases. The designated courts at present are Birmingham, Bristol, Cambridge, Canterbury, Cardiff, Carlisle, Exeter, Leeds, Manchester, Newcastle upon Tyne, Nottingham, Oxford, Plymouth, Southampton, Westminster and Wrexham County Courts.

Two people known as 'assessors' will be sitting with a judge hearing a race discrimination case. They are appointed by the Home Secretary and are supposed to have 'special knowledge and experience of problems connected with relations between persons of different racial groups'. However, the judge can sit alone if both sides agree to this. In any event, the decision reached at the end of the case is that of the judge alone.

Second, the appropriate court is usually the designated court for the district in which the discriminator lives or works or where the act of discrimination took place.

If you are not certain which is the right court to go to, inquire at the nearest County Court office. County Courts are usually listed in the telephone directory under 'Courts'.

Is there a time limit within which I must start proceedings?

If you are complaining about race discrimination in public-sector education (see page 69), you must start proceedings within eight months of the date on which the act of discrimination took place. In all other cases you must start proceedings within six months of the act of discrimination taking place. A month means a calendar month and in calculating the date on which the time limit expires, remember to include the date on which the discrimination took place as the first day of the relevant period.

If you apply to the Commission for Racial Equality (CRE) for assistance before the time limit has expired, then your time limit is automatically extended by two months. Thus it becomes ten months for public-sector education cases and eight months for all other cases.

The CRE normally has to let you know within two months of receiving your application whether or not they will grant you assistance. In some cases, the CRE might write to you within that two-month period and explain that they need a further month before they can reach a decision. If that happens, your time limit is further extended by one month. It is important that you keep that letter from the CRE in case it is later suggested that you started proceedings after the time limit had expired.

If you start proceedings after the expiry of the time

limit, the court may still hear your case if, in all the circumstances of the case, it considers that it is just and equitable to do so (see page 38).

Can I get more information before deciding whether or not to start proceedings?

Yes, you are entitled to ask the discriminator questions about the way you have been treated, the reasons for that treatment and any other questions which may be relevant. There is a standard form available free of charge from the CRE which you can use for the purpose of asking these questions. You do not have to use this form and can ask the questions in a letter if you wish to. You may, however, find it a lot simpler to use the standard form.

If you send the questionnaire to the discriminator *before* starting proceedings and within the time limit for starting proceedings, then your questions and the discriminator's replies become evidence in the case, and you can rely upon them in court. If the discriminator does not reply to your questions within a reasonable time, or the answers given are vague or evasive, the court is entitled to infer that you have been unjustly discriminated against.

If you have already started proceedings you can only serve questions upon the discriminator if the court gives you leave to do so. If it does, and you serve the questions within the period it specifies, then the questions and replies will be admissible as evidence.

The type of question you ask will of course depend upon the facts of your particular case. If you are not certain about what questions to ask or how to formulate them, seek assistance before doing so.

It is always useful to ask the questions before starting proceedings because it gives you a good indication of the strength of your case, which may be an important consideration in deciding whether or not to pursue it.

Can I get legal aid?

Yes, but in order to do so, you must:

(a) Convince the Law Society that it is reasonable for you to bring the proceedings. This eventually means that your case must be strong enough to merit it. If you have a weak or hopeless case, it is unlikely that you will get legal aid.

(b) You must also fulfil the financial requirements. Your income and capital must be below a certain level for you to qualify for legal aid.

You can get legal aid forms from solicitors, law centres, CABs (Citizens' Advice Bureaux), or the nearest Law Society's legal aid area office. The forms are fairly complicated to fill in, so if you don't have a solicitor get someone at the law centre or the CAB to help you complete one. If you don't know which solicitor you want to act for you, ask the law centre or CAB for their advice. They will know of solicitors who do legal aid work and possibly those who have some experience and expertise in the field of race discrimination.

After the forms have been sent, you will probably be called for an interview by the Department of Health and Social Security. It is their function to assess your financial situation and tell the Law Society the maximum you can afford to pay. It is important to attend this interview as failure to do so may result in your losing your right to legal aid.

Depending on your financial circumstances, you may get legal aid with 'nil contribution' (that is, you won't have to pay anything towards your costs), or you may not get legal aid at all, or you may get legal aid subject to your paying a certain contribution towards it.

Legal aid will cover all the expenses of having a

solicitor prepare your case and of having a solicitor or barrister represent you at the hearing itself.

If you are refused legal aid on the grounds that your case does not merit it, you can appeal to the legal aid area committee.

Can I get legal advice or assistance from anywhere else?

There are certain bodies which can provide you with advice, assistance and, in some cases, representation at court, without charging you anything:

The Commission for Racial Equality (CRE)
See pages 40–41 for the circumstances in which the CRE will provide assistance, and the ways in which it can assist you.

Law centres
See page 42.

Citizens' Advice Bureaux
See page 42.

Solicitors
See page 42.

Can I conduct a case myself?

Proceedings in a County Court are much more formal than in an industrial tribunal, and you will find it very difficult, if not impossible, to prepare and present your case without the service of a lawyer.

Before a case comes to trial, each side has to prepare documents briefly outlining the facts on which they rely and the course they wish the court to adopt. Each side can, if it thinks it necessary, ask the other to provide more details of the facts on which it relies. All these documents are collectively known as 'pleadings' and they are generally written in a fairly formal and legalistic style.

The procedure at the hearing itself is very formal and the rules of evidence are strictly adhered to. There are precise rules about evidence which is admissible and that which isn't, and it is very unlikely that a non-lawyer will be familiar with these. You will, therefore, be at a considerable disadvantage if you are conducting your own case.

If you do decide to conduct your own case, the following are a few useful tips:

(a) Proceedings are started by filling in a form called a 'request'. You can get this at any County Court office, and the staff there will help you complete it. Once this is done, the court will serve on the discriminator a summons stating that you are suing. You will also need to prepare a document called 'Particulars of Claim' which will briefly outline the facts upon which you rely and the remedy you are seeking.

(b) Have ready any document which is relevant and assists your case. Prepare two extra copies of all documents – one for the other side and one for the judge.

(c) Make sure that all your witnesses are willing to attend, and are available for the date of the hearing.

(d) Arrive at court in time for the hearing. If you cannot attend for any reason, for instance because you are ill, let the court know in advance.

Will I have to pay the other side's costs if I lose?
The general rule in the County Court is that the loser pays all the winner's costs. There are, however, two situations in which you won't have to pay the other side's costs if you lose. First, if you are assisted by the Commission for Racial Equality (CRE) and they have provided you with representation, they will pay the other side's costs. Second, if you were granted legal aid with 'nil contribution' it is extremely unlikely that the

court would order you to pay the winner's costs. If, however, legal aid was granted subject to your paying a certain contribution, then you may be ordered to pay the same amount as your contribution towards the other side's costs.

If the discriminator has engaged a solicitor and a barrister, it is likely that his costs will be quite substantial. Therefore, if you have not been granted legal aid and the CRE has refused your application for assistance, think long and hard before starting proceedings. Take advice from a law centre, a Citizens' Advice Bureau (CAB) or a solicitor (on the 'green form' scheme) on your prospects of succeeding before deciding whether or not to go ahead.

In what circumstances should I settle the case?

The same considerations apply when settling a case in the County Court as in the industrial tribunal (see page 45). The only additional factor, and it is an important one, is the question of costs. If there is a risk that you may lose the case, and therefore be ordered to pay the other side's costs, it would probably be advisable to accept a settlement. If at all possible try to get the other side to accept paying your costs as part of the settlement.

How do I prove discrimination?

As you are the person bringing the case, you have to satisfy the court on a balance of probabilities that you were racially discriminated against. 'On a balance of probabilities' simply means that it is 'more probable than not'.

Discrimination in a County Court is proved in exactly the same way as in an industrial tribunal – the court takes an identical approach to the tribunal in reaching its decision (see page 48).

What orders can the court make if I win?

In addition to declaring that the person in question has unlawfully discriminated against you, the court may order one or both of the following:

(a) An injunction to stop the person in question from discriminating unlawfully in the future. An injunction is an order of the court, and if the person disobeys it, he/she can be fined or imprisoned for contempt of court. These are not often granted by courts in discrimination cases.

(b) Damages. This is money given as compensation for any financial loss that you have actually suffered or are likely to suffer in the future. In addition, the court can compensate you for injury to your feelings. In most cases, the only damages you receive are for injury to feelings. The sum awarded for this varies according to the circumstances of your case and from court to court, but the average amount given nowadays is about £200 –£300. No damages will be awarded for indirect discrimination if it is proved that there was no intention to discriminate on racial grounds.

If you have incurred any costs in bringing the case, the court will order the other side to pay these. This would cover lawyers' fees (if you engaged any), court fees (you have to pay a certain amount for starting proceedings), witness expenses and any other expenses which you have reasonably incurred in bringing proceedings. If you were assisted by the Commission for Racial Equality (CRE), you won't receive any costs because you will not have incurred any expenses. Any costs awarded will go to the CRE, who will use it to pay your legal representation.

Can I appeal if I lose?

You can appeal to the Court of Appeal only if the judge misdirected him- or herself on the law or if there was no evidence to support the judge's findings of fact. A notice of appeal must be lodged within four weeks of the date on which judgement was given.

9: General Exceptions

What are 'general exceptions'?

In the preceding chapters we have looked at conduct which is unlawful in various spheres of your life – in relation to your work, education, housing, and the provision of goods, facilities and services. In each category, there were certain exceptions, that is, circumstances in which discrimination was permitted.

In addition, there are other exceptions which do not fall into any specific category but apply to all the areas we have considered. These have all been put together in this chapter and called 'general exceptions'. In some cases, the extent to which discrimination is permitted is limited, in others it is not and a general licence to discriminate is given.

The exceptions are broadly divided into the following four categories:

    (a) Sports and competition.
    (b) Government-related activity.
    (c) Acts safeguarding national security.
    (d) Charities.

We shall look at each of these in closer detail in the rest of this chapter.

To what extent is discrimination permitted in sport?

Discrimination in the selection of a team or in the rules relating to eligibility to compete in any sport or game is lawful if it is on the basis of your nationality or place of birth or the length of time for which you have lived in a particular place. It is, however, unlawful if it is on the basis of your colour, race or ethnic or national origins.

For example, a county cricket club is entitled to say that only people born in that county, or people who have lived in that county for five years, can be selected to play cricket for it. If you are a Pakistani, and have only lived in the county for three years, you cannot complain of race discrimination. If, however, you were born in the county and have lived there all your life, and the reason for not selecting you is your colour or the fact that your parents were not born in that county, then your treatment is unlawful and you are entitled to complain about it.

How is the government allowed to discriminate?
There are three ways in which discrimination by the government is lawful:

(a) It is lawful to pass discriminatory Acts in Parliament, and for Ministers to make discriminatory rules and regulations under that Act. Anyone who discriminates to give effect to them is not acting unlawfully.

Two simple examples illustrate how this works in practice. The Immigration Act 1971 and the rules made under it treat people less favourably on the basis of their nationality and, to an extent, their race and national origins. Non-EEC nationals coming to work in this country require a work permit in order to do so, and certain restrictions are imposed upon them as to where they can work. People from the Indian subcontinent who are settled in this country have to go through a rigorous procedure and a long waiting period before their families are allowed to join them here. You cannot complain to any court or tribunal about this discrimination because it is permitted. Similarly, the Minister for Education has made regulations which say that a student who has not been ordinarily resident in the UK for the three years immediately preceding the starting of a course is not entitled to a grant. Although this is indirect race discrimination, it is allowed. The same applies to charging higher fees to overseas students.

(b) Discrimination on the basis of nationality, place of ordinary residence or the length of time for which you have been present or resident in or outside the UK or an area within the UK is lawful if it is done to give effect to a circular or a directive of a Minister.

(c) There is no provision within the Race Relations Act 1976 under which you can complain if you have been discriminated against by government employees such as officers, police officers and prison officers. According to the law, they are not providing facilities or services to the public (which you might think they are) but are simply performing their duties.

What kind of discrimination is permitted to safeguard national security?

Once 'national security' is involved, discrimination is permitted on any basis in every sphere of your life. All that is required is a certificate signed by or on behalf of a government Minister certifying that an act was done for the purpose of safeguarding national security. No one is entitled to look behind the certificate and inquire why a certain act was necessary to safeguard national security. The Minister's certificate is conclusive evidence of the fact that it was.

The discrimination can be in any sphere of your life – employment, education, housing, access to goods, facilities and services; in employment, it is not limited to employment by the government as a public body, but applies equally to private employees.

The discrimination can be on the basis of your race, nationality, colour or ethnic or national origins. It is difficult to imagine how discrimination on the basis of colour (i.e. against black people) or ethnic origins (for example, against Jews) could ever be necessary to safeguard national security.

This exception gives the government wide and sweeping powers, but fortunately it is hardly ever used.

What is a 'charity'?

A charity is an institution or a trust which was set up to carry out purposes which are exclusively charitable. There is no exhaustive list of charitable purposes but it covers such things as the relief of poverty, advancement of education or religion, promotion of health, provision of recreational facilities and other purposes which are generally beneficial to the community. The benefits of the charity should be available to the public or to a section of it. There is a central register of charities which is open to the public.

When rich people die, they often leave their assets in a will or a trust for some specific charitable purpose. Thus institutions such as schools, hospitals, colleges and homes for the elderly or disabled are often set up and/or funded out of these assets. It is essential that the assets are used in such a way that they comply with the wishes of the person who gave them.

To what extent are charities allowed to discriminate?

When money is given for a charitable purpose, the class of people to benefit from it is usually defined in some way (it may be the old people in a certain area or students at a particular college). If the class of people is defined, amongst other things, by reference to colour, then effect will be given to the charitable instrument by ignoring the reference to colour. For example, a charitable trust gives scholarships to students at a college to study abroad. The terms of the trust are that it should

108

be given to white students born in the UK. The reference to 'white' will be disregarded, and the scholarship will be given to students born in the UK. If the class of persons is defined by reference to colour only, then the benefits will be given to persons generally.

If, however, a charitable body discriminates on one of the other racial grounds, for example on the basis of nationality or ethnic origins or by imposing a conditon which adversely affects persons of a particular racial group, effect can be given to that stipulation regardless of the race discrimination. Any person who discriminates against you in any sphere of your life, in order to give effect to it, is not acting unlawfully. Thus, a trust to set up a school with the specific condition that it should not admit anyone of the Jewish faith is permitted, and the head teacher of the school, in refusing a Jewish child admission, would not be acting unlawfully.

Thus, race discrimination is permitted by charities so long as it is not by reference to colour.

10: Other Unlawful Acts of Discrimination

Are there any other acts of discrimination which are unlawful?

We have so far looked at race discrimination which can have a direct effect upon you, and the legal action which you can take if you are the victim of such discrimination. In addition, there are other acts of discrimination which do not necessarily have an identifiable victim but are nevertheless unlawful. These are acts in respect of which you as an individual cannot bring any legal proceedings.

They fall into two categories. First, there are acts in respect of which only the Commission for Racial Equality (CRE) can take action. These can be summarized as discriminatory advertisements or practices, instructions and pressure to discriminate, and persistent discrimination. Second, there is the criminal offence of incitement to racial hatred for which an offender can be prosecuted in the criminal courts.

The rest of this chapter explains more fully these unlawful acts and the actions that can be taken in respect of them.

What kind of discriminatory advertisements are unlawful?

If you see an advertisement which indicates to you that someone intends to discriminate on racial grounds, and it does not fall into any of the exceptions below, it is unlawful. The exceptions (when discriminatory advertising is permitted) are:

(a) A job advertisement for persons of particular racial group when being of that racial group is a genuine occupational qualification for the job (see page 20).

(b) An advertisement for a job in this country, the purpose of which is to provide training in skills to be exercised outside Great Britain (see page 21).

(c) Advertisements by ethnic organizations (see page 94).

(d) Advertisements giving effect to the terms of charitable bodies (see page 108).

(e) Advertisements for facilities and services provided to persons of a particular racial group to meet their special needs (see page 93).

(f) Advertisements for the education and training of persons not ordinarily resident in Great Britain (see page 66).

(g) Advertisements for positive discriminatory training (see page 22).

(h) Advertisements for jobs in the civil service and public bodies which impose requirements relating to birth, nationality, descent or residence (see page 24).

(i) Advertisements for jobs overseas, so long as the persons to be employed are not defined by reference to colour, race or ethnic or national origins.

It is completely irrelevant where the advertisement appears. It could be a newspaper, magazine or some other publication; it could be broadcast on television or radio; it could be displayed on a notice, sign or showcard; it could be in circulars or catalogues or any other material which is distributed. Nor does it matter that the advertisement would not be seen by the public at large, but only by a select number of people. Thus discriminatory advertising in an in-house magazine, brought out by a company just for its staff, is unlawful.

The following are examples of advertisements which fall into the exceptions, and are thus lawful:

(a) An advertisement for a Chinese waiter to work in a Chinese restaurant.

(b) An advertisement for English classes for Bengali women.

(c) An advertisement for a Ministry of Defence job which stipulates that the applicant must be a British national.

(d) A department store advertising in an in-house magazine a training course for managers which is open only to the black sales assistants. This is lawful only if within the preceding twelve months there had been no black managers or the proportion of black managers was small in comparison with the proportion of black people employed by the store as a whole.

(e) An advertisement for engineers in Israel which stipulates that applicants must be Israeli nationals.

The following are examples of advertisements which are unlawful:

(a) An advertisement for white engineers to work on a project in South Africa.

(b) A notice in a newsagent's window for a flat to let which states 'no Blacks or Jews'. Although it is lawful for a landlord to discriminate in certain circumstances, (see page 77), advertising to that effect is, nevertheless, unlawful.

(c) An advertisement for 'a white nanny to look after two young children'. Again, although discrimination in jobs is allowed if the job is for the purposes of a private household, advertising which indicates that intention to discriminate is unlawful.

What can I do if I see a discriminatory advertisement?

Report the matter at once to the Commission for Racial Equality (CRE), giving as much detail of the advertisement as possible. If it appeared in a newspaper or magazine, send them a cutting of it with details of the name of the publication and the issue in which it appeared. If you saw the advertisement somewhere else, give as much detail as possible about its contents and about where and when you saw it. Remember to do this as soon as possible, because if the CRE are to take any proceedings in court in respect of it they must do so within six months of the advertisement appearing.

What are unlawful instructions to discriminate?

It is unlawful for someone who has authority over you or a special relationship with you whereby you normally do what they ask, to tell you to do anything which would amount to unlawful discrimination as described in Chapters 2–3 and Chapters 5–7. The actual words used by the person do not matter; it is irrelevant whether they amount to a formal command, a request, or the simple expression of a preference. What matters is the course of action which they are designed to bring about. If the result is going to be unlawful discrimination, then the instruction to you is unlawful. The following show the kind of instructions which are unlawful.

You are the manager of a night club, and have advertised for front doormen. The managing director calls you and says he would rather that you didn't employ any black people as that might put potential customers off. The managing director's instruction is unlawful even if, in the event, no black people applied for the job.

You work for an employment agency and have for many years supplied secretaries to a particular company. They are not satisfied with a black secretary you send, and thereafter instruct you not to send them any more black secretaries. That is an unlawful instruction.

What is unlawful pressure in discrimination?

It is unlawful for anyone to induce or attempt to induce another person to discriminate unlawfully in any of the ways described in Chapters 2, 3 and 5–7. The words 'to induce' do not have any special meaning, but simply mean 'to persuade or use influence on' or 'to cause or bring about'. The following are instances of unlawful pressure in discrimination:

The tenants on a particular housing estate petition their landlord, the local authority, not to allocate an empty flat on the estate to an Asian family.

The manager of a pub tells the clerk at a job centre not to send black applicants for the vacancy of bar-staff.

A hairdresser tells the careers service that black youngsters are not wanted as trainees under the Youth Training Scheme as the customers would object to a black trainee.

If someone is trying to persuade another person to discriminate, they are acting unlawfully even if they do not directly approach that person, but behave in such a way that that person is likely to find out about it. For instance, X distributes leaflets to residents asking them to voice their objections to the planning authority against applications by Asians for planning approval. Although X has not had any *direct* contact with the planning authority, the distribution of the leaflets is an attempt to induce the authority to discriminate in the provision of services, and is therefore unlawful. In such a situation X can also be prosecuted for the criminal offence of incitement to racial hatred (see page 117).

What can I do if someone instructs or attempts to induce me to discriminate?

Report the matter at once to the Commission for Racial Equality (CRE), giving as much detail as you can about what was said to you, by whom, and when. Remember, the CRE only has six months within which to bring proceedings.

If you lose your job for failing to comply with a discriminatory instruction, you can bring proceedings against your employers in an industrial tribunal on the grounds that they have discriminated against you because of someone else's colour (see page 8).

If you lose your job because you reported an unlawful instruction or inducement to the CRE, you can still bring proceedings in the industrial tribunal against your employers on the grounds that you have been victimized.

What action can the Commission for Racial Equality (CRE) take?

If the CRE has evidence about discriminatory advertising or instructions or pressure to discriminate, they can bring legal proceedings against the person responsible. If the advertising, instructions or pressure relate to employment, proceedings will be brought in the industrial tribunal. In any other case they will be brought in a County Court. Proceedings must be started within six months of the act taking place.

The CRE can ask the court or tribunal to do two things. First, they can ask it to give a ruling that the person concerned behaved unlawfully by publishing or causing to be published a discriminatory advertisement, or by instructing or pressurizing someone else to discriminate. Second, if they are of the view that the person concerned will continue to break the law in the same way, they can ask the court or tribunal to grant an injunction (a court order) to stop them from doing so in the future. If a person disobeys an injunction, they can be brought back to court for contempt of court, and can be fined or imprisoned.

What is a discriminatory practice and what can be done about it?

A 'discriminatory practice' is when someone imposes a condition or requirement which, if implemented, would result in indirect discrimination against a particular racial group, but it has not been challenged because there has never been an actual victim (see page 2 on indirect discrimination). For example, a factory has a rule that it will not employ anyone who wears a turban. No turbaned Sikh has ever applied to that factory for a job because it is well-known in the area that they won't employ anyone wearing a turban. Unless a Sikh applies for a job and is turned down, he cannot complain about the discriminatory condition.

If you know of anyone who is imposing a discriminatory condition or requirement, report the matter to the CRE. They can then conduct a formal investigation and, if satisfied that a discriminatory practice is being operated, they can serve a 'non-discrimination notice' on the person. This will essentially tell that person not to impose the discriminatory condition or requirement. If the notice is not complied with, the CRE can take legal proceedings and obtain an injunction (court order) to stop the condition or requirement from continuing to be imposed.

Is there anything to stop a person who has lost a case from continuing to discriminate?

If you bring a case in the industrial tribunal or the County Court and win, but fear that the person is going to continue to discriminate, report the matter to the CRE. You personally cannot take any legal proceedings to stop this person discriminating in the future, but the CRE can. If at any time within five years of you winning your case it appears to the CRE that the discriminator will continue to break the law, they can apply to the County Court for an injunction (a court order) restraining them from doing so.

Is it unlawful to make racist speeches or spread racist literature?

Yes. It is a criminal offence for anyone in a public place or at a public meeting to use words which are threatening, abusive or insulting and are likely to stir up hatred against any racial group in Britain. It is likewise a criminal offence for anyone to publish or distribute to the public at large or to a section of it written matter which is threatening, abusive or insulting and is likely to stir up racial hatred.

Thus the making of racist speeches is permitted at meetings of racist groups and organizations which are attended *only* by their members. Similarly, a racist group does not break the law if it distributes racist literature *only* among its own members.

It is entirely irrelevant whether the person responsible for the racist speech or the racist literature intended to stir up racial hatred or not; what matters is the effect that it was likely to have. If it was likely to stir up racial hatred, then the person in question has committed an offence.

If the material likely to stir racial hatred is contained in a fair and accurate report of either judicial proceedings or proceedings in Parliament then its publication and distribution is lawful. Thus, if a newspaper reports inflammatory and racist remarks made by a judge or a Member of Parliament, it does not break the law even though the reporting of those remarks is likely to stir up racial hatred.

What can I do about racist propaganda?

You as an individual cannot take any legal proceedings in respect of it; nor can the CRE. It is for the police and the prosecuting authorities to prosecute the offenders, but they can only do so if the Attorney General consents to it.

You can complain about it either to your local police station or to the CRE (the latter is usually likely to produce more results). If the CRE considers that a criminal offence has been committed, they will refer the matter to the Director of Public Prosecutions who advises the Attorney General. If the Attorney General refuses to authorize the bringing of proceedings, then that is the end of the matter. You cannot take any further action. The number of people complaining about racist propaganda has diminished over the past few years, mainly because they are disillusioned with the Attorney General's reluctance to bring proceedings.

What are the penalties for a person who is convicted?

That depends on where the person was tried. If the case was heard in the magistrates' courts, they can be fined up to £400 and/or imprisoned for up to six months. If the case was tried in the Crown Court they can be imprisoned for up to two years and/or fined any amount.

11: Commission for Racial Equality

What is the Commission for Racial Equality?
The Commission for Racial Equality (CRE) was set up in 1976 and it has the following duties:

(a) To work towards the elimination of discrimination.

(b) To promote equality of opportunity, and good relations between persons of different racial groups generally.

(c) To keep under review the Race Relations Act 1976 and to recommend amendments where necessary.

It consists of fifteen commissioners who are all appointed by the Secretary of State. One of these is appointed to be the chairperson, and two are appointed to be deputy chairpersons. The chairperson is a full-time appointment, the deputy chairpersons and other commissioners may be full-time or part-time appointments.

The CRE is funded entirely by the Home Office. Its budget for the 1985/6 financial year was £9,444,322. At the end of 1985 it had 200 permanent staff in post, eleven of whom were legally qualified. At least half of them were from ethnic minority groups.

The main office for the CRE is at:

Elliot House,
10/12 Allington Street,
London SW1E 5EH (telephone: 01-828 7022).

It also has offices at the following addresses:

Stanies House,
Fourth Floor,
10 Halliday Street,
Birmingham B1 1TG (telephone: 021-632 4544).

Maybrook House,
40 Blackfriars Street,
Manchester M3 2EG (telephone: 061-831 7782/8).

133 The Headrow,
Leeds LS1 5QX (telephone: 0532-34413/4).

What powers does the CRE have?

The CRE has powers to do the following:

(a) It can provide financial or other assistance to organizations concerned in the promotion of equality of opportunity and good relations between persons of different racial groups. Thus, it can give grants to community relations councils and other ethnic minority groups.

(b) It can undertake or assist research and educational activities concerned with race relations.

(c) It can issue codes of practice in the employment field, containing practical guidance on ways to eliminate race discrimination and promote equality of opportunity. The Code, accepted by Parliament in April 1984, is available from the CRE.

(d) It can conduct formal investigations. The investigation may be a wide and general one into a public activity, such as immigration or mortgage allocation, or it may be confined to a particular person who the CRE suspects may be discriminating. It can compel people who are under investigation to supply specific information and documents. Someone who conceals or destroys a document which they have been asked to produce, or who gives false information, commits a criminal offence and may be fined up to £400.

The CRE is obliged to prepare reports of their findings in formal investigations, and may make recommendations to any person that their practices or procedures should be changed so as to promote equality of opportunity between people of different races, or to the Secretary of State that changes in the law should be made to that end.

(e) It can issue non-discrimination notices. If in the course of a formal investigation the CRE becomes satisfied that someone is discriminating, they may serve a notice upon that person (a 'non-discrimination notice') telling him or her to stop breaking the law. If this means that practices will have to be changed, the CRE must be notified as to what the changes are and how they were made. The discriminator must take reasonable steps to make the changes known to the people whom they affect. In addition, the CRE may require the discriminator to supply them with certain information so that they can monitor compliance with the notice.

A person served with a non-discrimination notice may appeal against it within six weeks on the grounds that what they are required to do is unreasonable.

If a person fails to comply with a non-discrimination notice, the CRE can apply to the County Court for an order requiring him or her to comply with it. If that person persists in committing unlawful acts, the CRE can apply to the County Court for an injunction restraining them from doing so.

(f) In certain circumstances, the CRE can institute legal proceedings (see Chapter 10).

(g) It can provide assistance to individuals bringing proceedings in an industrial tribunal or a County Court (see pages 40 and 100).

(h) It can make representations to the Government on new legislation which is likely to affect race relations.

How has the CRE used its powers?

Between 1977 and the end of 1985, the CRE published reports on thirty-seven investigations which it conducted. Of these, seventeen related to employment, two to education, nine to housing and nine to the provision of facilities and services.

In 1985, the CRE spent about £140,000 on education and research, and gave in the region of £4 million to organizations concerned with race relations. It supported 176 cases of race discrimination. Of these, fifty-three were successful, fifty-eight were settled on agreed terms and sixty-five were dismissed after a hearing. The CRE took proceedings in fourteen cases of pressure and instructions to discriminate, and took action in thirteen cases of discriminatory advertisements. It referred ten complaints of incitement to racial hatred to the Director of Public Prosecutions. Five cases came for hearing during 1985. In three cases the defendants were acquitted. One case led to a conviction. In the fifth case, relating to *Bulldog* (the National Front Youth Magazine), one defendant was acquitted and the other was convicted.

Index

accommodation, *see* housing and premises
advertisements, unlawful, 110–12; procedure for, 112–13
armed forces, 24

Bank of England, 24
banks and building societies, 89–90
Bar Council, 32
British Association of Social Workers, 32
British Council, 24
British Medical Association, 32
Bulldog (National Front youth magazine), 122
business partners, discrimination by, 32–3

Central Office of Industrial Tribunals, 34–7
charities, extent of discrimination allowed to, 108–9
Citizens' Advice Bureaux, 41, 42, 99, 100, 102
Civil Aviation Authority, 24
civil servants, 23–4
clubs, 94
Commission for Racial Equality, 8, 10, 23, 31, 38, 40–41, 55, 57, 69–70, 73–4, 81, 97, 98, 100, 101, 102, 103, 110, 112–13, 114–15, 116, 117, 118, 119–22; definition of, 119; powers of, and use, 120–22
Community Relations Council, 10, 38, 62
'condition' or 'requirement', meaning of, 3
contract workers, 18
Council of Legal Education, 26
council tenants, 81–3
County Court, proceedings in, 17, 68, 77, 80, 83, 84, 92, 95, 96–104, 115, 116; circumstances for accepting settlement, 102; conducting your own case, 100–101; legal advice or assistance, 100; legal aid, 99–100; orders made, 103; payment of costs, 101–2; proving discrimination, 102; right of appeal, 103–4; time limit to start proceedings, 97–9; when to bring, 96; which County Court, 96–7
Crown Court, proceedings in, 27, 82, 118

Defence, Ministry of, 24, 112
definition of: Commission for Racial Equality, 119; discriminatory practice, and action to take, 116; employers, 12–13; general exceptions, 105; unlawful discrimination, 60–61; unlawful instructions to discriminate, 113; unlawful pressure in discrimination, 114
Department of Education and Science, 64, 69
Department of Health and Social Security, 99
direct discrimination, 1, 48–50
discriminatory practice, definition, 116

earnings, loss of, 53–4
education, 59–70; definition of unlawful discrimination, 60–61; further education, 64–5; lawful discrimination, 65–7; local education authorities, 67–8; procedure when discriminated against, 68–70; racial abuse or assault by other pupils, 61–2; racist books and teaching, 62; responsibility for race discrimination in schools, 63; teachers, discrimination against, 63
employers/employment, 12–33; application for a job, 14–16; armed forces, 24; civil servants, 23–4; contract workers, 18; definition of, 12–13; fellow employees, discrimination by, 19; genuine occupational qualification, 20–21; laws and, 13–27, 28–33;

123